IS THIS THE
ASIAN
CENTURY?

IS THIS THE

ASIAN

CENTURY?

Jong-Wha Lee
Korea University, South Korea

W **World Scientific**

NEW JERSEY · LONDON · SINGAPORE · BEIJING · SHANGHAI · HONG KONG · TAIPEI · CHENNAI · TOKYO

Published by

World Scientific Publishing Co. Pte. Ltd.

5 Toh Tuck Link, Singapore 596224

USA office: 27 Warren Street, Suite 401-402, Hackensack, NJ 07601

UK office: 57 Shelton Street, Covent Garden, London WC2H 9HE

Library of Congress Cataloging-in-Publication Data
Names: Yi, Chong-hwa, 1960–   author.
Title: Is this the Asian century? / Jong-Wha Lee.
Description: New Jersey : World Scientific, [2017] | Includes bibliographical references and index.
Identifiers: LCCN 2017027897 | ISBN 9789813227583 (hardcover)
Subjects: LCSH: Asia--Economic conditions--21st century. | Asia--Economic policy.
Classification: LCC HC412 .Y5175 2017 | DDC 330.95--dc23
LC record available at https://lccn.loc.gov/2017027897

British Library Cataloguing-in-Publication Data
A catalogue record for this book is available from the British Library.

Desk Editor: Jiang Yulin

Typeset by Stallion Press
Email: enquiries@stallionpress.com

About the Author

Jong-Wha Lee is a professor of economics and director of the Asiatic Research Institute at Korea University. He served as a senior adviser for international economic affairs to former President of the Republic of Korea. He was also previously Chief Economist and Head of the Office of Regional Economic Integration at the Asian Development Bank and an economist at the International Monetary Fund. He has taught at Australian National University, Harvard University and Peking University, and served as a consultant to the Harvard Institute for International Development, the Inter-American Development Bank, the United Nations Development Programme, and the World Bank.

He has published extensively on topics relating to human capital, growth, financial crises, and economic integration in leading academic journals. His most recent books include *Crisis and Recovery: Learning from the Asian Experience* (World Scientific, 2016), *Education Matters: Global Schooling Gains from the 19th to the 21st Century*, coauthored with R. J. Barro (Oxford University Press, 2015) and *Rebalancing for Sustainable Growth: Asia's Postcrisis Challenge*, co-edited with M. Kawai (Springer, 2015). He is a regular columnist for Project Syndicate and Korea JoongAng Daily.

He was awarded Chung-Ram Award (best young Korean economist) in 1997, Mae-Kyung Economist Award in 1997, and Dasan Economics Award in 2015. He is a president of the Korea International Economic Association. He obtained his Ph.D. and Master's degree in Economics from Harvard University.

Contents

Introduction

It was Spring of 2013 when I received an astonishing offer from Ken Murphy, the Editor-in-Chief of the *Project Syndicate*, to write articles at a regular basis for the *Project Syndicate* that I enjoyed reading. It is the ground where prominent policymakers and thinkers around the world deliver original and provocative commentaries on the world's contemporary issues in economics, politics, culture and society to global readers. Contributing my own columns regularly must serve an invaluable purpose, but at the same time must be challenging. Often, writing a short column is more difficult than producing an academic work as it requires more time and efforts to condense my knowledge and ideas into easily readable words.

Despite my initial hesitation, I accepted Ken's invitation. I agreed with Ken that it would be important that more Asian policymakers and thinkers, currently residing in Asia, participate in sharing their views and ideas not just about Asian but about global issues. To my thought, Ken and the *Project Syndicate* wanted to offer various sources and editorial assistance for the non-Western thinkers to raise their voices for the readers around the world. Since then, I enjoyed contributing my columns on the world's contemporary issues, focusing on Asian economies, for the "World's Opinion Page" where not many Asian columnists had performed.

A turning point of my professional career came when I took leave from Korea University and worked at the Asian Development Bank (ADB) for four years from 2007 to 2010. For most of my professional career, I focused on teaching students, writing technical journal articles, and sharing knowledge with other academics. However, during my tenure at the ADB, I had opportunities to communicate with a much broader audience, including policymakers, journalists and ordinary people who are unfamiliar with economic terms, on economic and social issues. To serve one of my duties as ADB's Chief Economist and spokesperson on economic issues, I met the audience via various media including presentations at Asian policymakers' meetings, media interviews, newspaper commentaries and explained current complex situations, prospects, and policy analysis on Asian economies in an understandable way. For instance, in early 2009 when the global financial crisis spread to Asia, I travelled in Asia and the United States to claim my economic reasoning on how Asian economies could manage a quicker V-shaped recovery than many had expected. In 2010, I had several formal and informal meetings with academics and policymakers in China to explain why Chinese economy could not continue growing at over 8% per year and advise them to strengthen macroeconomic management and implement structural reforms for soft-landing.

During my experience of working as a senior adviser for international economic affairs to President of South Korea for two years from 2011 to 2013, I was obliged to have a conversation with diplomats, journalists, and representatives of non-governmental organizations (NGOs). As a G20 (Group of Twenty) Sherpa (personal representative of South Korean President), I attended many G20-related meetings to discuss policy coordination among a group of major 20 (G20) economies. I emphasized the need of more active policies at national, regional and global level to resolve the financial crisis and help the world economy overcome prolonged stagnation and massive unemployment, and the need of expanding global trade and emerging and developing nations' growth potentials to create opportunities for the medium- and long-term sustained growth. I believe, in the time of global financial crisis, the information sharing and policy dialogues among regional and global leaders helped to reconcile different views of individual nations and produce some concrete outcomes for the world economy.

This book, *Is This the Asian Century?*, comprises 25 articles that I have published at the *Project Syndicate* since 2012. These articles are grouped into four broad topics:

- Part 1: Growth and Structural Adjustment
- Part 2: Economic Integration and Cooperation

- Part 3: Business, Money, and Finance
- Part 4: Education and Society

At the beginning of this millennium, an Asian century was a buzzword. Asia continued to raise its economic power in global production, trade and investment. With sheer population size and growing economic and political power, Asia appeared ready to overturn the world order and finally take center stage in the 21st century following the centuries of the Western dominance. However, in the wake of the global financial crisis in 2008–2009, Asian economies suffered from its spillovers and lost their faith in the sustainability of export-oriented development strategy.

In this light, this book explores whether the Asian Century is coming to pass or not and how Asian economies prepare for such century. I would like to share my analysis of Asia's economic transformation as well as social and cultural changes, and suggest the ways that Asian economies can overcome major economic and social challenges to continue their path toward a more balanced and sustainable growth in the 21st century. It is time to reset their growth model toward a new one that embraces financial stability, strong economic growth, income equality and environmental sustainability. As an author, I hope the columns in this book can provide useful knowledge and insightful ideas about Asian economies for global readers and contribute to ongoing policy debates on the future of Asian economies.

I am very grateful to Ken Murphy and the staff at the *Project Syndicate* for their support in improving my draft columns to be more readable and translating them into Chinese and other languages for non-English readers. I have also benefitted a great deal from discussions and editorial help from Young Chang and Eunbi Song. I also appreciate Hyein Cho and Yu-Jong Cho for their assistance in preparing the manuscript. I also appreciate the work of Jiang Yulin, and the editors of World Scientific who professionally managed the production and editing processes and expedited the publication of this book.

Part 1

Growth and Structural Adjustment

Safeguarding Asia's Growth*

Source: Patrick Foto / Shutterstock.com.

* Originally published in *Project Syndicate*, August 21, 2012.

Emerging Asian countries should be proud of their economic resilience. Despite a global economy plagued by weak growth, persistently high unemployment, and heavy debt loads, the region's emerging and developing economies grew at an average annual rate of 6.8% from 2000–2010, propping up global output and buttressing recovery efforts.

The region's success has been underpinned by dynamic growth in China and India, which account for almost 60% of the continent's total GDP in purchasing power parity terms. Furthermore, economic-policy changes and structural reforms that were enacted in the wake of the 1997–1998 Asian financial crisis significantly reduced the region's vulnerability to financial shocks over the past decade.

But Asia cannot be complacent: financial systems remain fragile; economies are burdened with high fiscal and current-account deficits; and Asia remains too heavily dependent on North American and European export markets, increasing its vulnerability to external shocks.

Moreover, if conditions in the eurozone continue to deteriorate, Asia could be more severely affected. Already, spillover effects from trade and financial transmission channels are beginning to take their toll: China's GDP growth rate in the second quarter of 2012 averaged 7.6%, reflecting a significant slowdown, and India's growth rate is expected to decline to roughly 6% this year.

China's potentially strong domestic-demand base and ample room for policy maneuvers can help it to avoid a hard landing. It has already aggressively loosened monetary policy, and it can employ further fiscal stimulus. But policy mismanagement and structural weaknesses in the financial sector and local governments could undermine efforts to safeguard growth.

Meanwhile, India, constrained by a high fiscal deficit and persistent inflationary pressure, has less scope for expansionary policies and faces significant challenges in pursuing credible structural reform.

This has serious implications for the rest of Asia. Over the last three decades, increased economic and trade integration has bolstered the region's growth. For example, segmented production for global supply chains has stimulated trade in intermediate goods and promoted foreign direct investment. Now, however, closer economic integration means that sluggish growth in China and India will reduce job opportunities and slow the rate of poverty reduction throughout the region.

Faced with weak demand in advanced countries, Asian economies are working to rebalance their sources of growth by shifting toward domestic and regional markets. As a result, growth in intra-regional trade has outpaced overall trade growth, with intra-Asian trade now accounting for more than half of the continent's total trade turnover.

But China's established role as the assembly hub for the region's production-sharing networks means that it is becoming a source of autonomous shocks — with a large and persistent impact on business-cycle fluctuations.

So, what policies must emerging Asian economies pursue to reduce their vulnerability to regional and global volatility?

The most immediate challenge is to safeguard the financial system's stability against external shocks. Policy reform should aim to promote market transparency, improve risk management, and strengthen effective supervision and regulations.

Second, emerging countries must develop more effective macroeconomic frameworks, including better macro-prudential regulation and a broader monetary-policy framework that takes into account asset prices and financial-market stability. A wide range of official measures could be employed to support domestic demand while protecting medium-term fiscal sustainability. And, to address volatile capital flows, countries should increase exchange-rate flexibility, maintain adequate international reserves, and implement carefully designed capital controls.

Third, emerging economies must further rebalance their sources of growth. Reducing dependence on external demand — for example, by promoting private-sector investment and encouraging household expenditure — is crucial. Supply-side policies that promote small and medium-size enterprises and service industries accommodating domestic demand are also critical to ensuring more inclusive and sustainable growth.

Finally, enhanced regional and global financial cooperation — including closer policy coordination at the G-20 and International Monetary Fund — would help countries to respond more effectively to shocks and crises. A key regional initiative is the $240 billion multilateral reserve pool of the

ASEAN+3 (the Association of Southeast Asian Nations plus China, Japan, and South Korea), which can provide short-term liquidity to members when needed. Institutional arrangements in regional liquidity provision and economic surveillance must be enhanced.

Asians need not be pessimistic; the perfect storm of a hard landing in China, a double-dip recession in the United States, and a collapse of the eurozone is unlikely. But they cannot rule out the downside risk of a synchronized global downturn. Only with preemptive policies designed to manage risk better can emerging Asian countries protect economic growth from the threat of current and future crises.

Abenomics and Asia*

Source: alexmillos / Shutterstock.com.

*Originally published in *Project Syndicate*, April 8, 2013.

Japanese Prime Minister Shinzo Abe's economic agenda — dubbed "Abenomics" — seems to be working for his country. Expansionary monetary policy is expected to inject liquidity into the Japanese economy until inflation hits the Bank of Japan's 2% target, while expansionary fiscal policy is expected to continue until economic recovery takes hold.

As a result, consumer and investor confidence is returning. The Japanese stock market has soared more than 40% since November of last year, when it became clear that Abe would form the next government, and exports and growth are also picking up. With a large output gap and low inflationary pressure, expansionary policies show great potential for reviving economic activity.

But other countries — including neighboring Asian economies — fear that Japan is devaluing the yen to bolster exports and growth at their expense. Some have accused Japan of fueling a global "currency war." Anticipation of aggressive monetary expansion has sharply weakened the yen, which has fallen by almost 20% against the dollar in just over four months.

Of course, Japan's escape from its 15-year deflationary trap and two decades of economic stagnation would be good for the world. Japan remains the world's third-largest economy, the fourth-largest trader, and the third-largest export market for neighboring China and South Korea, which thus stand to benefit if "Abenomics" revitalizes Japanese domestic demand. More broadly, given Europe's slide into recession and only a slow rise in world trade volume, renewed growth and stronger import demand in Japan would support global recovery.

The question now is whether Abenomics can achieve its goals without destabilizing the world economy, especially neighboring Asian economies. Doing so requires Japanese policymakers to focus on more sustainable growth while averting a vicious cycle of competitive devaluation and protectionism with Japan's trade partners. In particular, expansionary monetary and fiscal policies — which are helpful in the short term — must be accompanied by fundamental structural reforms.

Japan's deflation and economic stagnation over the last two decades stemmed largely from a dysfunctional financial system and a lack of private demand. The collapse of asset bubbles in the 1990's left Japan's financial system and private sector saddled with a huge debt overhang. Recovery began only after the balance-sheet weaknesses in the financial, household, and corporate sectors were addressed. Sustainable growth requires sustained private-sector demand.

Monetary easing and fiscal stimulus, combined with structural measures to restore private firms to financial health, would stimulate household expenditure and business investment. Indeed, the impact of real exchange-rate depreciation on growth is likely to be short-lived unless increased corporate profits in the export sector lead to higher household consumption and investment. And yet risks to financial and fiscal stability could arise if higher inflation and currency depreciation were to spoil investors' appetite for Japanese government bonds, thereby pushing up nominal interest rates.

That is why the success of "Abenomics" hinges not on the short-term stimulus provided by aggressive monetary expansion and fiscal policies, but on a program of structural reform that increases competition and innovation, and that combats the adverse effects of an aging population.

Japan, of course, is not alone in using exchange-rate policies to keep exports competitive. Many emerging economies' authorities intervene in currency markets to prevent exchange-rate appreciation and a loss of export competitiveness. But if Japan starts to intervene directly in global currency markets to ensure a weaker yen, neighboring competitors will respond in kind. The danger of a currency war and protectionism should not be underestimated.

In South Korea, the government and business leaders worry that a stronger won, which recently rose to its highest level against the yen since August 2011, will hurt key export sectors, including automobiles, machinery, and electronics. One report by a Korean research institute shows that the Korean economy will slip into recession if the yen-dollar exchange rate nears 118, its average level back in 2007.

Moreover, unlimited quantitative easing by the Bank of Japan, the Federal Reserve, and the European Central Bank also increases the risk of volatile capital flows and asset bubbles in Asian emerging economies. Chinese policymakers have raised serious concerns about the growing risks of inflation and property bubbles.

This delicate situation could escalate into further currency intervention, trade protectionism, and capital controls. Beggar-thy-neighbor policies could lower total trade volume — a zero-sum game from which no one would benefit. After all, Japanese exports rely on emerging and developing markets, with East Asia alone accounting for nearly half of Japan's foreign sales.

The regional economy would benefit from closer coordination of exchange-rate and monetary policies. Mechanisms like the G-20 and ASEAN+3 (ASEAN, with China, Japan, and South Korea) should be used more actively for policy dialogue and surveillance. East Asian economies could then, over time, cooperate to enhance regional exchange-rate stability, thereby creating a more conducive environment for intra-regional trade.

Japan's economy is moving at last, which bodes well for Asia and the world. But, despite its new vigor, the benefits of recovery could prove to be short-lived unless a sustainable and cooperative growth path is found.

Asia's Rebalancing Act*

Source: Image Team / Shutterstock.com.

*Originally published in *Project Syndicate*, September 23, 2013.

Rapid economic growth in China undoubtedly benefits the rest of Asia. Indeed, strong Chinese demand has supported its trading partners' export-led growth for much of the past three decades. But now, faced with a slowdown in China and significant downside risks there, the rest of Asia must abandon over-reliance on export-oriented development strategies and strive to ensure stable and sustainable growth domestically and regionally.

China's vulnerabilities and risks — stemming from property bubbles, shadow banking, and local-government debt — have triggered concerns about a crisis not only there, but also in neighboring Asian countries. Some, indeed, now predict a Chinese banking or fiscal disaster; others predict long-term stagnation equivalent to Japan's lost decades.

These "hard landing" scenarios are extreme. But the road ahead is bumpy and uncertain. No one can guarantee that Prime Minister Li Keqiang's attempts to achieve deleveraging and structural reform will succeed. Moreover, external shocks, policy mistakes, and political instability could disrupt even the best-laid plans.

In any case, China's stellar growth record cannot be sustained. Even if it manages a "soft landing," annual output growth will slow to 5–6% in the coming decades. Standard growth theory predicts "convergence" of *per capita* GDP: a fast-growing country will eventually encounter difficulty maintaining high rates of labor mobilization, capital accumulation, and technological progress.

In China, labor inputs have fallen as a result of declining fertility and an aging population. Reduced rates of return will lower investment rates. China may be able to rely on policy reforms to boost productivity growth; but, with relatively low innovative capacity, it will struggle to catch up with frontier technologies.

China's inevitable growth slowdown, along with a large tail risk, threatens stable growth in Asian economies that have become increasingly interdependent. Trade within Asia now accounts for more than half of the continent's total trade turnover. Moreover, direct investment and financial flows contribute further to economic interdependence.

The rise in intra-Asian trade reflects China's central role in East Asia's production networks. From 2001 to 2011, China's share of South Korean exports doubled, from 12% to 24%; its share of Japanese exports grew even faster, rising from 8% to 20%. As a result, China has become South Korea's single largest export market, and Japan's second largest. It is also the largest trading partner of all ten members of the Association of Southeast Asian Nations (ASEAN).

Asian economies' deepening trade and financial integration has left them increasingly vulnerable to growth shocks from China, with exporters of commodities and capital goods especially vulnerable. In fact, a study[1] by the Asian Development Bank shows that Chinese shocks have larger and more persistent effects on individual Asian economies' output than do global shocks, as a 1% increase in China's GDP raised GDP in emerging East Asia by about 0.6%.

In terms of investment, the International Monetary Fund predicts[2] that a disruption in China's investment boom will adversely affect its trading partners. A drop of one percentage point in China's investment rate is estimated to reduce Taiwan's GDP growth rate by 0.9 percentage points and Korea's by 0.6 percentage points.

If China can successfully rebalance its economy and shift to consumption-based growth, its trading partners could benefit enormously from a huge retail market. But as long as China's import share of final consumption remains low, direct gains for exporters of consumer goods are likely to be small.

As they prepare for the coming Chinese slowdown and seek to minimize the risk of regional destabilization, Asian economies must strengthen domestic demand and reduce excessive reliance on exports to China. In other words, sustainable growth requires all of Asia's China-dependent economies to rebalance their two main growth engines.

To enhance domestic demand, Asia, including China, must reallocate resources and structurally transform the economy. Reinforcing social safety nets, broadening and deepening financial markets, and supporting small and medium-size enterprises would also strengthen domestic demand. Likewise, service-sector liberalization will be essential to promoting productivity and creating jobs. In short, implementation of fiscal, financial, and structural reforms can mitigate the spillover effects from China's slowdown.

But a second reform front, aimed at enhancing regional coordination, must also be opened. With economic shocks able to spread more quickly than ever before, owing to broadened trade and financial channels, all Asian countries must maintain a sound macroeconomic environment.

Perhaps most important, deeper regional integration calls for closer cooperation in macroeconomic and financial surveillance, as envisaged by the Chiang Mai Initiative Multilateralization. Asian countries must be able to conduct well-coordinated candid reviews of one another to reduce the likelihood of risks and detect emerging vulnerabilities.

China's long-term growth potential — and that of the rest of developing Asia — is not pre-defined. Maximizing it requires not only that individual countries address their weaknesses and rebalance their sources of growth, but also that they build and strengthen the regional institutions needed to manage economic integration.

India's Chinese Dream*

Source: xtock / Shutterstock.com.

---

*Originally published in *Project Syndicate*, July 24, 2014.

In recent years, China and India have both emerged as global economic superpowers, with China leading the way. But, with Chinese growth slowing and the need for structural change becoming increasingly acute, will the economic-reform efforts of India's new prime minister, Narendra Modi, enable the country to catch up?

Since the 1980s, China has experienced unprecedented economic growth,[1] fueled by abundant low-cost labor, high saving and investment rates, substantial market reforms, outward-oriented policies, and prudent macroeconomic management. Its leaders now hope to achieve high-income status by developing more technologically sophisticated industries.

India's economic performance has been less remarkable. Economic growth began to accelerate dramatically in the early 1990s, owing to trade liberalization and other economic reforms. Then reforms stalled, the fiscal and current-account[2] deficits soared, and annual GDP growth fell to 4–5%.[3]

As a result, China has pulled ahead, with per capita income last year standing at $11,850 — more than double[4] India's $5,350. The question now is whether Modi's push for faster growth can narrow the income gap in the coming decades.

The most important factor working in India's favor is its "demographic dividend." In China, population aging and low fertility rates are already causing the prime working-age population, people aged 15–59, to decline. From 2015–2040, this group is expected to shrink by more than 115 million.[5] Meanwhile, India's prime working-age population will increase by 190 million.

But favorable demographics alone will not bring about the kind of growth that has made China the world's second-largest economy. India's leaders must develop a comprehensive plan to eliminate barriers to economic competitiveness, expand employment opportunities in manufacturing, and improve workers' education and skills.

As it stands, India ranks 60th in the world[6] for economic competitiveness — much lower than China, which, at 29th, is closing in on high-income countries like South Korea (25th) and France (23rd). The reasons for this are not difficult to discern: India performs poorly on the fundamental drivers of long-term economic prosperity.

Indeed, despite steady improvements, public health and education levels remain low (102nd worldwide). Moreover, the lack of adequate transport, communication, and energy infrastructure (85th) is undermining India's productivity growth. And India lags behind China in the efficiency of its product and labor markets (ranking 85th and 99th, respectively). Only by addressing these shortcomings can India attract sufficient investment and boost economic growth.

At the same time, India should expand labor-intensive manufacturing, thereby creating employment opportunities for its growing pool of workers. Given that manufacturing contributes only 15% of India's total output,[7] compared to 31% in China, there is considerable room for growth.

In a sense, India has the advantage of being able to learn from China. China transformed its agrarian economy by building a strong, labor-intensive industrial base, shifting workers from agriculture to manufacturing and construction, and improving productivity across all sectors. Today, the agricultural sector accounts for only one-third of total employment[8] in China, compared to one-half in India.

India's structural transformation and sustainable growth will hinge on its efforts to build a flexible labor market, centered on the easing of outdated and complicated employment laws. The legal protections of workers in India's formal sector exceed those of most developed countries, as well as China, with mandated requirements rising as the number of employees increases. As Jagdish Bhagwati[9] and Arvind Panagariya[10] have pointed out, excessive labor-market regulations deter Indian entrepreneurs from employing unskilled workers and developing labor-intensive manufacturing, implying that the Indian government should redouble its reform efforts in this area.

Equally important, Indian workers — especially young people — need opportunities to upgrade their skills continuously. The McKinsey Global Institute estimates[11] that, of the potential global oversupply of 90 million low-skilled workers in 2020, 27 million will be in India. Meanwhile, the country will face a shortage of 13 million medium-skilled workers.

Despite India's educational expansion, especially at the secondary and tertiary levels, its system of higher education, including technical and vocational education and training, remains inadequate. Though India's public vocational education and training systems are well institutionalized, they lack the scale, curriculum, financing, and incentives needed to prepare young workers to meet the demands of rapid globalization and technological advancement.

The good news is that Modi seems committed to boosting India's competitiveness by improving its business climate. For example, he has already announced measures to promote foreign direct investment in insurance, defense, and telecommunications, including higher infrastructure spending and new tax incentives for savings and investment. India's government will also sustain its predecessors' efforts to strengthen vocational education and skills training.

What Modi's plan lacks is a strong focus on expanding India's labor-intensive industries. That, together with the planned reforms, would enable India to seize the opportunities that arise with favorable demographics and achieve Chinese-style growth.

Starting South Korea's New Growth Engines*

Source: ESB Professional / Shutterstock.com.

*Originally published in *Project Syndicate*, January 26, 2015.

In the last half-century, South Korea has become a model for developing countries, with remarkable economic growth enabling it to
become the world's eighth largest trading country and achieve *per
capita* income of \$26,000.[1] But lately its economy has been faltering, with
GDP growth averaging 3.6% for the last ten years — a significant drop
from the 8.1% annual growth rate that prevailed in 1965–2005. And the
OECD projects[2] a further decline — to around 2.5% — in the coming
decade.

But a forecast is not fate. With a new economic strategy that nurtures
more diversified sources of growth, while reducing the country's excessive reliance on exports and large enterprises, South Korea can
reinvigorate and sustain strong growth.

South Korea's economic performance over the last 50 years was
attributed largely to good fundamentals, including a high savings rate,
strong human capital, sound institutions, and prudent fiscal and monetary
management. Trade openness provided access to inexpensive imported
intermediate goods, larger markets, and advanced technologies, thereby
contributing to rapid productivity growth in the country's manufacturing
industries. Performance-based incentives facilitated the continuous
upgrading of South Korea's comparative advantage in global markets.

The problem is that such policies have led South Korea to become
excessively dependent on exports for growth. Exports accounted for about
56% of South Korea's gross national income in 2013, compared to 34%
in 2002 and just 15% in 1970. As a result, South Korea's economy has
become highly vulnerable to changes in external demand — a fact that
became starkly apparent during the 2008 global economic crisis.

South Korea's relationship with China perfectly illustrates the challenges it faces. As China's economic growth soared, so did its share of
South Korea's total exports, which doubled, from 12% to 24%, in the
period from 2001 to 2013. But China's economy has recently begun to
slow, and its growth trajectory is expected to be much less steep in the
coming years than it was over the last three decades.

Moreover, China is posing increasingly tough competition for South
Korea, by encouraging the emergence of more technologically advanced
industries like electronics, information technology, motor vehicles, semiconductors, shipbuilding, and high-end steel products. China's efforts to

upgrade its own growth model, together with the possibility of long-term stagnation among advanced economies, raise serious concerns about South Korea's prospects.

Compounding these problems is the wide imbalance between South Korea's manufacturing and services sectors. Though services account for 76% of employment,[3] its contribution to overall economic growth is small, owing to low productivity. Indeed, value added per worker in the services sector remains just 40% of that in the manufacturing sector, and annual productivity growth was only 2%[4] from 1980 to 2010 — significantly lower than the manufacturing sector's rate of 8.2%.

Against this background, South Korea's new growth strategy should aim to achieve both a demand-side rebalancing and supply-side productivity increases.

On the demand side, South Korea must begin by boosting household expenditure. This will require reversing the sharp decline in the proportion of middle-income households,[5] which is down to 67.5%, from 75.4% in 1990. With more than half of these households earning less than they spend every month, household debt has been rising fast, and now stands above 160% of disposable income — one of the highest levels in the OECD. Transferring unused corporate savings to households, while reducing the number of low-wage temporary and part-time workers, would boost domestic demand and reduce income inequality.

Policies aimed at increasing female labor-force participation and lowering private education spending would also help. At the same time, South Korea should work to improve the investment climate to raise the quantity and quality of investment, particularly of small- and medium-size enterprises (SMEs) in the services industry.

On the supply side, structural reforms to stimulate productivity growth[6] could, for example, emphasize the development of modern services industries, including health care, education, telecommunications, business processing, and legal and financial services. Efforts to ease product regulations and lower barriers to foreign investment would promote competition and technological innovation.

South Korea must also dismantle the obstacles that start-up businesses face. To this end, the government must redress shortcomings in the venture-capital market, nurture the labor force's skills, and encourage entrepreneurship. It must also confront the huge, family-controlled *chaebols* — such as Hyundai, LG, and Samsung — that contributed significantly to rapid industrialization and technological advancement but also block competition from start-ups and SMEs, stifling dynamism and innovation. Stricter rules are needed to improve corporate governance and prevent unfair practices by those affiliated with the *chaebols*.

South Korea is at a crossroads. Though President Park Geun-hye's administration, which took office in 2013, has unveiled many economic initiatives to foster a "creative economy," their effect so far has been minimal. But her government still has three years to pursue reforms that support the emergence of the services sector, start-ups, and SMEs as South Korea's new growth engines, capable of powering a more dynamic and innovative economy for the next 30 years.

Containing China's Slowdown*

Source: Project Syndicate.

* Originally published in *Project Syndicate*, September 23, 2015.

Pundits love debating the Chinese economy's growth prospects, and nowadays the pessimists are gaining the upper hand. But many are basing their predictions on other economies' experiences, whereas China has been breaking the mold on economic growth for the last three decades. So, are China's economic prospects as bad as prevailing wisdom seems to indicate? And, if they are, how can they be improved?

China's situation is certainly serious. The economy grew by 7.4% last year, the lowest rate since 1990; it is unlikely to meet the official target of 7% this year, and, according to the International Monetary Fund, will probably grow by a mere 6.3% in 2016.[1] Clearly, weak domestic activity and diminished external demand are taking their toll.

China is also losing long-term growth momentum, as falling fertility rates and returns on investment weaken labor-force expansion and capital accumulation. And it is becoming increasingly difficult for China to take advantage of technology-driven productivity gains.

All of these challenges have led former US Treasury Secretary Lawrence Summers[2] and his Harvard colleague Lant Pritchett to argue[3] that China's growth could slow to 2–4% over the next two decades, as the country succumbs to the historically prevalent growth pattern implied by "regression to the mean." But, given that China's growth pattern has, so far, been exceptional, the notion that it will suddenly start following a common trajectory seems unlikely.

Similarly flawed is the view[4] of Justin Lin, former Chief Economist of the World Bank. Lin argues that China can achieve 8% annual growth for another two decades, owing to its enduring "latecomer advantage," which, among other things, entails rapid productivity gains brought about by technological catch-up with the United States. But this fails to account for the standard growth theory of "conditional convergence": only economies with comparable structural characteristics, such as labor skills and institutional quality, converge to similar *per capita* income levels.

For these reasons, I take a more moderate view,[5] predicting that China's average potential GDP growth will fall to 5–6% by 2030. This expectation is based on a conditional convergence framework that relies on data generated by China's unique growth experience, as well as those of other economies, over the last three decades.

Unlike Lin, I believe that China's inevitable economic slowdown is coming soon. But, unlike Summers, I do not believe that it has to be dire. The key to this scenario is that China's leaders move the economy onto a more balanced and sustainable growth path, based on realistic expectations. They cannot afford to mishandle unavoidable challenges, such as those stemming from domestic institutional weaknesses, political uncertainty, and external shocks.

The first step in any effective strategy must be to recognize that, in such a large and unpredictable economy, the government cannot rely on direct intervention or macroeconomic policies. Instead, it must implement reforms that boost productivity and offset downward pressure on growth.

Reforms in factor markets — labor, land, and finance — are essential. China's leaders must improve labor-market flexibility and labor mobility; make land use, acquisition, and compensation more efficient; and build a more market-based financial system.

As it stands, China's financial system is highly regulated and dominated by banks, many of which are state-owned. To change this, the government needs to promote market-based credit allocation. China needs a flexible and efficient financial sector, underpinned by an effectively supervised and regulated capital market, to avoid asset bubbles and support productive and innovative firms.

Similarly, policies to promote continuous technological innovation and industrial upgrading can increase productivity. And measures that increase domestic research capacity — for example, by strengthening protection of intellectual property rights — can nurture innovation.

Reform of China's massive state-owned-enterprise (SOE) sector would also boost productivity. The recently announced SOE reforms are a promising step. Beyond promoting mixed ownership involving private capital, strengthening corporate governance, and facilitating commercial operations, the reforms promise to open up the energy, resources, and telecom industries to non-state investors. This new round of SOE reform should be pursued diligently.

Such efforts to increase productivity are all the more important as China moves to shift from investment- and export-led growth to a more sustainable model based on domestic consumption and services. Reallocating resources from export-oriented industries to service activities could cause an irreversible drop in productivity.[6] Likewise, while policies that encourage firms to increase wages will raise household income and domestic consumption, wage increases can erode export competitiveness and choke off inflows of foreign direct investment. With rebalancing policies alone unlikely to increase average output growth substantially, enhancing productivity is crucial[7] to China's long-term prosperity.

The final piece of the puzzle for China is realism. As it stands, the Chinese government is keen to maintain decent growth of about 7% annually while pushing for rebalancing and reform. The risk is that, until reform measures take effect, the authorities may rely on short-term stimulus to meet growth targets, aggravating resource misallocation and structural vulnerabilities. Considering that China's total debt reached 282% of GDP last year — surpassing America's debt level — further reckless lending to local governments and private enterprises from the shadow banking sector would hold the economy hostage to the growing risk of a financial crisis.

To avoid such an outcome, China should lower its growth target to about 6% in the coming years. That way, it could pursue the deep reforms that are needed to move the economy onto a more balanced and sustainable long-term growth path.

Is South Korea Turning Japanese?*

Source: Project Syndicate.

---

* Originally published in *Project Syndicate*, November 17, 2015.

South Korea's recent economic performance has been disappointing. After 40 years of astonishing 7.9% annual GDP growth, the average growth rate dropped to 4.1% in 2000–2010, and has stood at a mere 3% since 2011. This has many wondering whether South Korea is headed for the kind of protracted deflation and stagnation that characterized Japan's so-called "lost decades," from which it is just beginning to emerge.

The similarities between South Korea today and Japan 20 years ago are undeniable. And, in fact, on economic matters, South Korea has, for better or worse, often followed Japan's example. In this case, Japan's example can save South Korea — if, that is, South Korea's leaders take it as a lesson in what not to do.

Japan's woes are rooted in real-estate and equity bubbles, which were fueled by monetary expansion aimed at stimulating domestic demand after the 1985 Plaza Accord[1] drove up the yen's value and hurt Japan's exports. In the early 1990s, the bubbles burst, leaving the private sector with a huge debt overhang. Add to that sluggish productivity growth, weak demand, and rapid population aging, and Japan's situation was dire.

At first, Japan's authorities turned again to fiscal and monetary expansion. But fiscal policies often targeted unproductive projects, such as rural infrastructure construction, and weaknesses in the banking system dampened the effectiveness of monetary stimulus. As a result, the economy grew by just 1.1%, on average, in the 1990s, far below the 4.5% of the 1980s.

In the early 2000s, Prime Minister Junichiro Koizumi's government took aggressive action to tackle underlying problems in the financial and corporate sectors. Despite these efforts — not to mention the boost provided by rapid GDP growth in China, Japan's economy expanded by just 0.75% annually, on average, for the entire decade.

Things have been looking up since Prime Minister Shinzo Abe[2] took office in 2012 and launched his three-pronged recovery strategy, dubbed "Abenomics," which entailed bold monetary easing, fiscal expansion, and structural reforms. Stock prices have climbed more than 80%. The yen's depreciation — from ¥78 to ¥123 against the US dollar — has boosted exports of industrial products and, in turn, corporate profitability. Consequently, employment and wages have also increased.

Now, Abe is preparing to augment these efforts with initiatives to address major drags on Japan's economy. So-called "Abenomics 2.0" entails efforts to raise the fertility rate (free preschool education, support for fertility treatments, and greater assistance for single-parent families) and to mitigate problems associated with population aging (boosting social security and providing more employment opportunities for retirees).

But Japan's economy is by no means out of the woods. On the contrary, GDP contracted by 0.1% last year, and is expected[3] to grow by just 0.6% this year. Moreover, despite continued purchases of ¥80 trillion per year in government bonds, the Bank of Japan has failed to achieve its 2% inflation target. And Japan's public debt-to-GDP ratio, at 240% (and rising), remains the highest in the world.

And Abenomics 2.0 may not succeed, not least because young people, unconvinced that they can support larger families, are increasingly delaying marriage and children. Against this background, many believe that preventing the current population of 127 million from falling below 100 million — Abe's official goal — will require Japan to accept more immigrants. That is no small matter in a country that places such a high value on homogeneity.

Simply put, while Japan has some reason for hope, its position is not enviable. And, if South Korea is not careful, it could end up in much the same place.

Employing many of the same development strategies — including export-oriented policies and a conglomerate-dominated industrial system — South Korea has been catching up with Japan for four decades. Its *per capita income*[4] (in terms of purchasing power parity), just one-fifth of Japan's in 1970, amounts to almost 95% of Japan's today. Over the same period, South Korea's share of global exports[5] jumped from 0.3% to 3% — very close to Japan's 3.6%.

To be sure, significant differences between the two countries remain. South Korea still lags behind Japan in international influence and institutional quality. South Korea ranks 26th on the World Economic Forum's Global Competitiveness Index,[6] whereas Japan ranks sixth. Based on the gap in GDP per worker with that of the US, South Korea is more than 20 years behind Japan.

Nonetheless, the reality is that South Korea has been experiencing many of the same problems Japan did in the early 1990s, including high levels of household and corporate debt, labor- and financial-market inefficiencies, and low productivity in the service sector. Given a fertility rate of just 1.2 births per woman — among the lowest in the world — South Korea's labor force is set to shrink by a quarter by 2050, with people aged 65 and over accounting for 35% of the total population, up from 13% today. This will put serious strain on public budgets.

If South Korea is to avoid Japan's fate, it must take steps to reduce its household and corporate debt. It also should continue to implement structural reforms aimed at strengthening its labor and financial markets, improving institutional quality, and boosting productivity in services and small and medium-size enterprises.

Taking a cue from Abenomics 2.0, South Korea would do well to provide a better environment for child rearing, including flexible working environments, affordable and high-quality childcare and after-school programs, and paid maternal and paternal leave. Financial support, such as low-interest loans for newlyweds, could also promote marriage and childbirth.

Japan's lost decades highlight the importance of treating economic ills with the right medicine, before they become chronic and difficult to cure. If South Korea takes this lesson, and implements the right policies and reforms, being like Japan won't have to mean sharing its economic fate.

Maintaining the Emerging-Economy Growth Engine*

Source: Nerthuz / Shutterstock.com.

---

*Originally published in *Project Syndicate*, March 16, 2016.

The world's emerging economies seem to be losing their dynamism. Countries that only a few years ago were being hailed for their resilience in the face of a global economic meltdown are now facing myriad challenges, reflected in significantly slower GDP growth. Is the emerging-economy growth engine breaking down?

From 2000 to 2007, annual growth[1] in emerging and developing economies averaged 6.5%. More impressive, from 2008 to 2010, when the advanced economies were in recession or struggling through a fragile recovery, they managed to sustain 5.5% growth.[2] In fact, at the end of that period, average growth stood at a very healthy 7.5%.

But then growth began to slow, with the annual rate falling to 4% in 2015. Even China, the largest and most dynamic emerging economy, recorded its lowest growth rate since 1990 (6.9%) last year, and the slowdown is forecast to accelerate this year. Many now argue[3] that the emerging economies are settling into a "new normal" of slower growth, and that their days as the key driver of the global economy are over.

Despite their current struggles, it would be premature to write off the emerging economies. For starters, even if these countries' growth rates do not return to pre-crisis levels, their contribution to the world economy should remain substantial, given that their share of world GDP[4] in purchasing-power-parity terms has increased significantly, from 43% in 2000 to 58% in 2015.

But the emerging economies have much more to offer. With the right policies, they can tap into as-yet-unexploited growth potential and continue their progress toward convergence with advanced-economy income levels. The key to determining what those policies must be is to understand why growth has slowed in the first place.

At first, emerging economies were hit by external challenges, including weakening world trade, low commodity prices, and tight financial conditions. Global merchandise trade slowed considerably over the last four years; in the first half of 2015, it contracted[5] for the first time since 2009. Oil and metal prices[6] have dropped more than 50% from their 2011 peaks.

Moreover, the US Federal Reserve's monetary-policy reversal,[7] which entails a long-delayed increase in interest rates, combined with the negative-interest-rate policies of the Bank of Japan and the European Central Bank, has caused financial-market fluctuations and left emerging economies vulnerable to capital flight. These external factors could be cyclical, but it remains to be seen how soon they will pass.

The recent emerging-economy slowdown is also the result of structural factors.[8] When the emerging economies' growth stories began, the gap between their actual *per capita* incomes and long-run potential enabled rapid capital accumulation and strong technology-enabled productivity gains.

But after years of large-scale investment — which, in China in particular, has led to excess capacity and resource misallocation — capital accumulation has moderated. Meanwhile, as countries move closer to the technology frontier, imitation and adaptation must give way to genuine innovation — no easy feat when innovative capabilities are lacking. So what can emerging economies do to improve their prospects? Though the particular policy mix will vary by economy, some priorities are clear.

For one thing, countries must strengthen their resilience against adverse external shocks, including through efforts to strengthen their own financial systems. To reduce their vulnerability to volatile capital flows, they should promote exchange-rate flexibility, secure adequate international reserves, and adopt carefully designed capital controls.

Emerging economies that rely excessively on exports need to rebalance their sources of growth toward domestic demand. Investment in public infrastructure, an improved investment climate, and social safety nets could all help to spur higher private-sector investment and household expenditure.

Greater priority must also be given to structural supply-side policies targeting productivity growth. First, to strengthen human capital, emerging economies must complement their progress in educational attainment with efforts to improve schools' quality, especially at the secondary and tertiary levels. Where necessary, education systems must be reformed to meet changing industry demand and skill requirements.

Second, structural bottlenecks[9] must urgently be addressed, through the streamlining of regulations, as well as reforms to promote competition in product markets and to increase the flexibility and efficiency of factor markets for labor, finance, and land. Emerging economies must lower barriers to market entry, support business operations, and increase access to finance. Obstacles to trade and foreign direct investment must be removed as well.

Finally, emerging economies must work to strengthen their institutions. As it stands, corruption[10] — facilitated by complex and burdensome regulatory environments, inefficient tax regimes, and weak judicial systems incapable of protecting investor and property rights — is pervasive in many emerging economies, hindering sustained growth. Improving governance and bolstering the rule of law are essential to boosting productivity[11] and long-term GDP growth.

The emerging-economy growth engine is not broken; it simply needs to be serviced. With appropriate policies and structural reforms, the emerging economies can recapture their dynamism and move onto an even stronger growth path — taking the entire global economy with them.

How Slow Will China Go?*

Source: dibrova / Shutterstock.com.

---

*Originally published in *Project Syndicate*, July 18, 2016.

C hina's economic performance over the last few decades has been outstanding. Despite possessing very different institutions than those seen in the advanced economies, no doubt a result of its communist system, China managed to achieve[1] 8.7% average annual *per capita* GDP growth from 1980 to 2015. The key has been its unique strategy of "crossing the river by feeling the stones," whereby it has gradually tested, implemented, and adjusted reforms and growth-enhancing policies.

But, while China's economic development has been exceptional in many ways, its growth performance is not unique. Both Japan and South Korea also transformed their economies through rapid industrialization and export-oriented policies, backed by strong investment, before experiencing slowdowns. If China is to manage its current challenges — in particular, sharply decelerating growth — it should look to these countries' experience for guidance.

All three countries have followed a similar path, but at a different time. Based on *per capita* GDP, China is more than 40 years behind Japan

Asia's Growth Paths
Per capita GDP and GDP growth rates, select countries

Key: Bubble size = GDP growth rate (%)

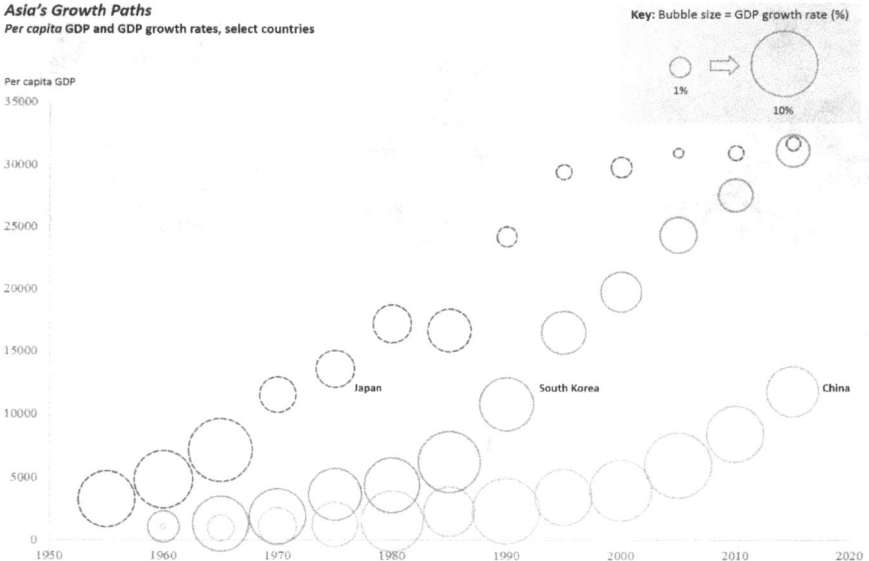

Notes: left axis is *per capita* GDP in 2005 international prices; bubble size *per capita* GDP growth rates, 5-year avg (%)
Source: Penn World Table 9.0

and about 20 years behind South Korea. Specifically, Japan's annual *per capita* GDP growth averaged 8.6% in the 1960s, before plummeting to 3–4% in the 1970s and 1980s. South Korea's GDP growth dropped from 7–8% in the 1970s and 1980s to 4% in the 2000s. China's three-decade-long run of double-digit growth came to an end in 2010, with the annual rate now below 7%. In each case, the decline in growth came when *per capita* income reached about $8,000.

The growth trajectory experienced by these three Asian countries can be explained by the "convergence" phenomenon — the tendency of poor countries to grow faster than rich countries, once they address certain structural and policy factors. The economic logic of this "catch-up" process is straightforward: for countries with lower levels of *per capita* output, there is a larger gap between current and potential capital stock and technology.

That gap can be closed rapidly through the adoption and imitation of existing technologies, which improve productivity, and through high rates of accumulation of physical capital, owing to higher returns on investment. And, indeed, Japan, South Korea, and China all maintained high levels of investment throughout the catch-up process, peaking at nearly 40% of GDP in Japan in the 1970s. South Korea reached similar levels in the 1990s; and China's investment spending currently stands[2] at more than 45% of GDP.

As countries move closer to their potential *per capita* output levels, the power of convergence diminishes, forcing its beneficiaries to adjust their growth models accordingly. Reducing investment, due to its lower returns, is an important component of that adjustment. Another is increasing technological innovation, to avoid a sharp slowdown in productivity growth. A third is shifting output from low-value-added agricultural and manufacturing goods to higher-value-added domestic services.

China, like Japan and South Korea before it, is now pursuing this adjustment. But it faces serious obstacles, beginning with limited institutional and human capabilities — a constraint that could hinder domestic innovation and efficient resource allocation. China also faces diminishing labor input growth, owing to low fertility rates and rapid population aging. According to the United Nations, the average growth rate of the working-age population[3] will be –0.1% in 2010–2020, a sharp decline from 1.5% in 2000–2010.

In addition, as employment moves to the services sector, overall productivity growth could fall, as it did in Japan and South Korea. In China, GDP growth per worker in the services sector[4] was only 1.3% in 1981–2010, compared to 15.1% in the manufacturing sector.

Of course, China should not be working to restore past rates of GDP growth. That would be a waste of time. As former US Treasury Secretary Lawrence Summers[5] and Harvard University professor Robert Barro[6] have pointed out, a slowdown was inevitable for China, just as it was for Japan and South Korea. My work[7] suggests that China's GDP growth rate will decline to 5–6% in the coming decade, and 3–4% in the long run.

With its catch-up glory days in the past, China should aim for higher incomes through steady growth and lower volatility. To achieve this, it must focus specifically on crisis prevention and management. That is where Japan and South Korea went wrong.

In the 1980s, Japan allowed asset bubbles to grow. That may have spurred growth for a while, but when the bubbles burst, the financial system's huge debts helped push the economy into a bout of deflation and stagnation from which it has still not fully emerged. Similarly, South Korea was thrown into financial crisis in 1997, when panicked foreign investors fled, hitting the over-leveraged corporate sector hard as the air was sucked out of the under-supervised financial system.

As it stands, China seems to be moving along a similar path. According to the Bank for International Settlements, Chinese corporate debt has increased rapidly[8] in recent years, from 99% of GDP in 2008 to 166% in 2015, with more than half of the debt owed by poorly performing state-owned enterprises (SOEs). This does not bode well for the corporate sector or the financial system.

But it is not too late to change course. To avert a crisis, China's leaders must act now to address the weaknesses in the corporate and financial sectors and to improve macroeconomic- and financial-policy frameworks. To keep productivity — and incomes — rising, they must continue to implement structural reforms that support labor-market flexibility and the development of human capital, while privatizing SOEs and liberalizing the financial sector.

Like its neighbors, China will have to confront slower growth, and its social consequences, head-on. But the country's future is anything but predetermined. With the right approach, it can manage a smooth transition from middle- to high-income status — a transition that would not only improve the wellbeing of China's 1.3 billion citizens, but also reduce risks and uncertainties in the global economy.

Part 2

Economic Integration and Cooperation

Euro Lessons for East Asia*

Source: Igoror / Shutterstock.com.

*Originally published in *Project Syndicate*, December 5, 2012.

East Asia could learn two valuable lessons from the eurozone crisis. First, do not rush the process of financial and monetary integration; and, second, develop adequate institutional frameworks before proceeding.

In fact, East Asian countries are unlikely to move toward a regional fixed exchange-rate system or a monetary union with a single currency in the immediate future, owing to the region's great diversity in terms of economic and political conditions. Perhaps, in a few decades, the region's countries will develop institutions to promote financial integration, such as a single bank supervisory agency of the type that the European Union is now creating.

Nevertheless, Asian policymakers should improve cooperation mechanisms designed to prevent and manage crises. Most promising is the Chiang Mai Initiative Multilateralization (CMIM)[1] of the ASEAN+3 — the 10 members of the Association of Southeast Asian Nations plus China, Japan, and South Korea. This $120 billion regional reserve pool was launched in 2010 to provide short-term liquidity to members in an emergency.

The ASEAN+3 is now strengthening the CMIM by doubling the total fund size to $240 billion. The group also agreed to enhance the CMIM's flexibility by reducing the minimum portion of crisis lending to be tied to the International Monetary Fund's lending program from 80% to 70%.

The CMIM has yet to be tested in a crisis. In its infancy, it might not be able to provide adequate emergency support in a timely and flexible manner. The $240 billion fund is small, amounting to only about 1.5% of the region's GDP. European experience suggests that large-scale systemic shocks call for greater financial support.

Unlike the IMF or the European Stability Mechanism, CMIM contributions are self-managed by the respective country's authorities. And countries may choose not to contribute to a swap request. This suggests that the CMIM could be especially constrained amid a systemic shock or political disputes among member countries.

Moreover, an "IMF stigma" remains among those countries in the region that were discontented with the Fund's role during the 1997–1998 Asian financial crisis. IMF conditionality for the activation of the majority of their borrowing could make countries reluctant to turn to the CMIM for support.

Another challenge is the CMIM's limited capacity for economic surveillance and monitoring. Last year, ASEAN+3 established a regional surveillance unit, the ASEAN+3 Macroeconomic Research Office (AMRO),[2] to monitor regional economies, detect emerging vulnerabilities, and support effective decision-making by the CMIM. But it is unclear whether AMRO has sufficient capacity and expertise to monitor 13 countries effectively.

Indeed, East Asian countries may find it difficult to conduct candid surveillance of one another's policies and enforce firm policy conditionality. The example of Greece before and during the eurozone crisis shows that it is often hard for countries to be tough on their neighbors.

The ASEAN+3 must continue to increase its resources, enhance its independence and improve its operational procedures. A fully capable regional financial safety net could contain the contagion of financial shocks emanating from individual economies and prevent disruptions to the region's key growth drivers — intra-regional trade and investment. The CMIM could help East Asian countries to reduce their reliance on accumulating, as a form of self-insurance, costly reserves that fuel global imbalances.

With greater resources and an improved governance structure, AMRO could play a more effective role in regional economic surveillance and monitoring, without which moral-hazard risks associated with financial safety nets would rise. Enhanced regional control would contribute to better information-sharing and decision-making as well, implying that the IMF-linked portion of CMIM crisis lending could be reduced in step with the strengthening of AMRO's capacity and performance.

The ASEAN+3 should aim to develop the CMIM into a full-capacity regional financial safety net supported by AMRO as a capable and credible secretariat — a *de facto* Asian Monetary Fund, possibly with broader membership. But, until the CMIM and AMRO are fully developed, their close cooperation with the IMF is desirable. Indeed, at the Cannes G-20 Summit in November 2011, leaders agreed on principles for cooperation between the IMF and regional financing arrangements, including open information-sharing and joint missions.

In particular, the IMF and ASEAN+3 financing arrangement should establish a regular channel of dialogue to facilitate information exchange and prepare concrete guidelines for cooperation and an appropriate division of tasks. Establishing constructive and effective guidelines could help to prevent the sort of conflicts and confusion over lending conditions during crises that we have seen among the IMF, EU, and the European Central Bank in the eurozone. Given the "IMF stigma" in Asia, a co-financing facility that provides precautionary credit lines without policy conditionality to qualified member countries would be useful.

Asian countries have learned from their region's own crisis in the 1990's, as well as from the eurozone's ongoing crisis, that effective management of cross-border capital flows requires well-constructed national, regional, and global responses. To respond effectively to crises, East Asian countries must continue to improve the regional financial safety net and surveillance mechanism, while strengthening their cooperation with the IMF.

Financial Safety Nets for Asia*

Source: retrorocket / Shutterstock.com.

* Originally published in *Project Syndicate*, November 12, 2013.

E merging economies are facing significant uncertainty and serious downside risks. One major source of instability is the looming reversal of the US Federal Reserve's expansionary monetary policy — the prospect of which is generating volatility in global financial markets and threatening to disrupt emerging-economy growth.

The Fed has signaled that its federal funds rate will remain near 0%, at least as long as unemployment exceeds 6.5% and inflation expectations remain well anchored. But when and how the Fed will begin tightening monetary policy remains unclear. What is certain is that, in making its decision, the Fed will not consider its policy's spillover effects on the rest of the world, leaving affected countries' policymakers and central bankers to deal with the fallout.

Tighter US monetary policy could intensify the global credit shortage, thereby increasing pressure on Asia's economic and financial systems. Overreaction and herding behavior by market participants could trigger a sudden reversal of capital inflows, with a severe dollar shortage — as occurred in 1997 and 2008 — straining Asian banks and corporations.

These risks explain why the Fed's mere suggestion of a potential move toward reducing its purchases of long-term asset (so-called quantitative easing) caused emerging-market currencies and asset prices to plummet this summer. They also underscore Asian economies' need for stronger financial safety nets.

The 2008 global financial crisis revealed fundamental flaws in the international monetary system, as the failure to ensure sufficient liquidity weighed heavily on emerging Asian economies. Since then, these countries have taken measures to safeguard the stability of their financial systems against volatile external shocks, strengthen financial supervision and regulation, and develop more effective macroeconomic frameworks, including better macro-prudential regulation and capital-control measures. But their heavy reliance on international trade and capital flows means that they remain vulnerable to severe financial spillovers from the United States.

Moreover, since the 1997 Asian financial crisis, the region's emerging economies have increased their holdings of foreign-exchange reserves, and now possess more than half of the world's total. Seven of the world's top ten reserve-holding economies are in Asia. But hoarding international reserves, mostly in the form of low-yielding short-term US Treasury securities, is expensive and inefficient.

Some Asian economies, especially China, are also attempting to internationalize their currencies. Given China's expanding global influence, the renminbi's emergence as a new international currency is inevitable. For smaller economies, however, internationalization will be far more difficult.

In their quest to ensure sufficient liquidity, Asian economies have also actively pursued currency-swap arrangements. Since 2008, China has signed 23 bilateral swap agreements, including one with South Korea. Japan expanded bilateral swap facilities with its Asian neighbors during the global financial crisis. And the ten ASEAN countries, together with China, Japan, and South Korea, have constructed a $240 billion regional reserve pool to provide short-term liquidity to members in an emergency.

Such swaps should help Asian countries to cope with currency turmoil in the wake of a Fed policy reversal. But they remain untested and, given their relatively small volumes, cannot reassure markets or provide adequate emergency support to crisis countries, especially in the event of large-scale systemic shocks.

The Fed, as the *de facto* global lender of last resort, can improve significantly the effectiveness of Asia's financial safety nets by establishing currency-swap arrangements with emerging economies' central banks during the policy-reversal process.

In 2008, the Fed established currency-swap lines with the central banks of ten developed economies, including the eurozone, the United Kingdom, Japan, and Switzerland, and four emerging economies (Brazil, South Korea, Mexico, and Singapore). These arrangements, most of which ended in 2010, responded to strains in short-term credit markets and improved liquidity conditions during the crisis. The South Korean central bank's $30 billion swap, though limited, averted a run on the won.

Reestablishing the Fed's swap arrangements with emerging economies would minimize negative spillovers during the coming monetary-policy reversal. Even an announcement by the Fed stating its willingness to do so would go a long way toward reassuring markets that emerging economies can avert a liquidity crisis.

The swap lines would also serve American interests. After all, trouble in emerging economies would destabilize the entire global economy, threatening the fragile recoveries of advanced economies, including the US. And, given China's rise, it is clearly in America's interest to maintain a balance of economic power in Asia.

Critics might cite the moral-hazard risk generated by liquidity support. But a well-designed framework that offers swap lines only to well-qualified emerging economies — and only temporarily — would diminish this risk substantially.

In fact, some experts, such as the economist Edwin Truman, have proposed establishing an institutionalized global swap arrangement[1] as a more effective and robust crisis-prevention mechanism — an idea that G-20 countries should consider. But creating such a system would take time. In the meantime, the Fed should take the initiative by re-establishing swap lines with advanced and emerging economies alike.

Is North Korea Opening for Business?*

Source: Evlakhov Valeriy / Shutterstock.com.

*Originally published in *Project Syndicate*, January 16, 2014.

North Korea's system is failing. The country is facing severe energy constraints, and its economy has been stagnating since 1990, with annual *per capita* income, estimated at $1,800,[1] amounting to slightly more than 5% of South Korea's. Meanwhile, a food shortage has left 24 million North Koreans suffering from starvation, and more than 25 of every 1,000 infants die each year, compared to four in South Korea.[2] In order to survive, the world's most centralized and closed economy will have to open up.

A more dynamic and prosperous North Korea — together with peace and stability on the Korean Peninsula — would serve the interests not only of North Korea itself, but also of neighboring countries and the broader international community. After all, North Korea's sudden collapse or a military conflict on the peninsula would undermine regional security, while burdening neighboring countries with millions of refugees and hundreds of billions of dollars in reconstruction costs.

This should spur international institutions and North Korea's neighbors to provide the food aid, technical assistance, and direct investment that the country needs to escape its current predicament and make the transition to a market economy. But there remain significant obstacles to such cooperation — not least the North's obscure and often-unpredictable politics, exemplified by the recent execution of its leader Kim Jong-un's once-powerful uncle, Jang Song-thaek.

The good news is that North Korea's leadership seems to understand that its current troubles stem from its grossly inefficient economic system. In recent speeches, Kim has emphasized the need for economic reform and opening up to develop agriculture and labor-intensive manufacturing industries.

Furthermore, in a bid to attract foreign investment, the government has announced the establishment of 14 new special economic zones. If only out of a sense of self-preservation, North Korean political and military leaders are likely to support this effort, as long as it does not undermine their power or national security.

Officially, North Korea began opening up to foreign investors in 1984, when the government enacted the Foreign Joint Venture Law, following the success of a similar law in China. In 1993, North Korea continued this effort by establishing the Rajin-Sonbong special economic and trade zone.

But these initiatives have yet to yield significant results, with foreign investors wary of operating in a country that lacks both economic-policy credibility and the physical and institutional infrastructure needed to support large-scale projects.

North Korea now should follow the examples of Vietnam and China, pursuing reforms like deregulation, liberalization, privatization, and macroeconomic stabilization, while developing a new legal system and new institutions. Such market-based, outward-oriented economic policies are a prerequisite for long-term economic growth.

The country certainly does not lack growth potential. While North Korea does not have the agricultural base that initially spurred reforms in China and Vietnam, geographical advantages like natural seaports and rich mineral resources enable it to pursue export-led growth.

Moreover, the relative abundance of well-educated workers implies low initial wages and the ability to compete internationally in labor-intensive manufacturing activities — for example, in footwear, textiles and garments, and electronic assembly — which can form the basis for export-led industrialization. To this end, a significant share of North Korea's military manpower, which currently amounts to more than 8.5% of the total labor force, could be used for more productive purposes.

If the relevant conditions are satisfied, North Korea could capitalize on the "catch-up" effect, boosting growth further, because its low *per capita* income level would help to increase investment productivity and facilitate technology transfer from more developed economies.

This implies a significant role for North Korea's neighbors, especially South Korea and Japan. So far, however, the Kaesong Industrial Complex, operating with about 50,000 North Korean workers under South Korean management, is the only case of economic cooperation between the two Koreas.

North and South Korea are natural trading partners. In 2012, inter-Korean trade amounted to $2 billion — only 0.2% of South Korea's total trade, but 29% of North Korea's. According to the economist Marcus Noland, normalized trade relations could increase South Korea's share of the North's trade volume to as much as 60%.

With a strong commitment to economic reform and opening up — backed by robust international support — North Korea could emulate the success of East Asian economies like South Korea, experiencing annual growth of more than 5% for the next several decades.

But there is more to North Korea's situation than economics. The country is locked in a stalemate with the international community, which wants it to denuclearize and become a "normal" country. Unwilling to abandon its nuclear-weapons program, North Korea faces economic sanctions from the United States, with official aid and membership in institutions like the World Bank and the International Monetary Fund on hold.

Given how unlikely North Korea is to denuclearize, at least in the immediate future, an alternative strategy is needed. The international community, especially South Korea, should support North Korea's efforts to build a more open, market-based economy through expanded trade and investment, while continuing to work toward a compromise on denuclearization. The resulting prosperity and accessibility could, over time, bring about political change.

For ordinary North Koreans, who are suffering the most under the current system, such a transformation could not be more urgent.

China's New World Order*

Source: humphery / Shutterstock.com.

---

*Originally published in *Project Syndicate*, November 12, 2014.

China — already the world's largest exporter, manufacturer, and international-reserve-asset holder — is poised to overtake the United States as the world's largest economy (measured according to purchasing power parity) this year. Now, it is using its growing clout to reshape global economic governance. Indeed, the country's days of following Deng Xiaoping's injunction to "hide brightness and cherish obscurity" are long gone.

After decades of actively participating in international economic institutions — including the G-20, the International Monetary Fund, the World Bank, and the World Trade Organization — China has begun to resemble a revisionist power seeking to create a new world order. Last month, China and 20 other Asian countries signed a memorandum of understanding[1] to establish a new multilateral development bank, the Asian Infrastructure Investment Bank. Viewed as the first serious institutional challenge to the World Bank and the Asian Development Bank (ADB), the AIIB was proposed by China.

In a sense, this shift should not be surprising, given the widespread debate over the inherent weaknesses of existing international institutions and governance structures — in particular, China's disproportionately small role in them. China accounts for a 3.8% voting share of the IMF[2] and a 5.5% share of the ADB,[3] compared to 16.8% and 12.8%, respectively, for the United States and 6.2% and 12.8% for Japan.

Moreover, the advanced economies have staked their claim to leadership in these institutions. Europeans have led the IMF and Americans have controlled the World Bank since their establishment after World War II. Likewise, the ADB has had Japanese presidents since its founding in 1966.

Meanwhile, emerging economies like China face significant barriers to boosting their capital contributions to — and their status in — these institutions. And reforms, though widely discussed, have faced long delays. For example, IMF quota and governance reform,[4] on which G-20 leaders agreed in 2010, has yet to be implemented.

Frustrated, China finally decided to push for the establishment of the AIIB, in which it will be the largest shareholder, with a stake of up to 50%. China will also provide the AIIB's first president, and the bank's headquarters will be in Beijing.

China can leverage its considerable influence over the AIIB to bolster its international image, particularly by strengthening its relationships with developing countries. Many developing Asian countries, for example, have significant unmet need for infrastructure investment to buttress their long-term economic growth.

The AIIB can not only channel more resources toward developing countries; it can do so in a way that is better suited to their needs, with fewer bureaucratic barriers and more flexibility than its more established counterparts. The AIIB would complement China's rapidly increasing bilateral development financing, with the added benefit of a multilateral structure that ensures better governance and higher operating standards.

What the AIIB may not be able to do is contribute to improved economic governance in Asia — not least because Japan, Australia, Indonesia, and South Korea, whose total GDP is roughly equal to China's, are not yet members. Without these economies to counterweigh China's influence or a resident board of directors, the AIIB could allow China to impose its will on members and beneficiaries alike.

For example, as former Indian Minister of State for External Affairs Shashi Tharoor[5] has suggested, China may use the AIIB to help finance a new Silk Road,[6] an overland and maritime route connecting East Asia with Europe. While the project could have significant regional benefits, stimulating economic development by promoting integration and connectivity, it would serve primarily China's interests, expanding the country's international influence and reducing the gap between its eastern and western regions. At the same time, it could exacerbate geopolitical tensions and territorial disputes between China and its neighbors.

More generally, some development experts have raised concerns[7] about whether the AIIB can operate according to international standards of governance and transparency, enforce safeguards, refuse to work with incompetent or corrupt governments, and follow effective procedures. They also worry that, by fragmenting international development finance, the AIIB could weaken its impact considerably.

To be sure, China has made an effort to address such concerns, emphasizing repeatedly that the AIIB aims to complement, not compete with, other institutions. Following the AIIB's launch, Chinese President Xi Jinping declared[8] that it "needs to follow multilateral rules and procedures" and should learn from "existing multilateral development institutions in their good practices and useful experience."

But China must support such statements with an active commitment to fair and efficient governance. Specifically, it should consider lowering its own voting share, instituting a rotating presidency, and broadening membership to include advanced Asian economies.

The AIIB is a welcome initiative. But, given deep mistrust and a multitude of conflicts involving China, its regional neighbors, and the United States over security, environmental, and human-rights issues, its success is far from guaranteed. It is up to China to make the necessary compromises to enable the AIIB to reach its potential.

China's approach to influencing global governance is only beginning to emerge. One hopes that it starts off on the right foot.

Uniting for an Asian Century*

Source: Lisa Kolbasa / Shutterstock.com.

* Originally published in *Project Syndicate*, November 21, 2016.

There is no question that Asia's standing in the global economy is stronger than ever. The region now produces about 40% of the world's GDP,[1] measured according to purchasing power parity. During the recent economic crisis, Asia accounted for more than half of global GDP growth. Add to that a massive population and growing political influence, and Asia finally appears ready[2] to lead on a world stage long dominated by the West.

But it is too early to open the champagne. The United States and Europe maintain an advantage, in terms of global strategic influence, while Asian countries are facing major political, economic, and security challenges.

In fact, Asia's growth momentum is declining. China is working overtime to achieve an economic soft landing, following decades of breakneck expansion. Japan is preoccupied with escaping slow growth and coping with population aging. Asia's other economic powerhouses — India, Indonesia, and South Korea — each face their own set of economic and political problems. Across the region, rising income inequality, financial instability, and environmental degradation are hampering development.

More problematic, despite being deeply interdependent, the region's countries struggle to act collectively. The persistence of power rivalries, historical resentments, and territorial disputes, together with pronounced disparities in economic and military might, create substantial obstacles to unity. A recent surge in coercive behavior by China, a nationalist revival in India, and a shift toward conservatism in Japan have exacerbated these challenges.

But, at a time when Western countries are moving toward isolationism — exemplified by the Brexit vote in the United Kingdom and the election of Donald Trump as US president — intra-regional trade and investment are more important than ever. Beyond the economic benefits, integration would yield important political benefits, with an integrated Asia enjoying more influence on the international stage. To reap those benefits, Asia must mitigate regional military and political conflicts and develop a long-term vision for regional integration.

Asia is home to some of the world's most dangerous flashpoints. There is a risk of armed clashes in the East and South China Seas, and North Korea continues to develop nuclear weapons[3] and ballistic missiles, despite tougher sanctions pushed by the United States and the United Nations. Stronger cooperation among Asian countries, together with the international community, could ease regional tensions and lead North Korea to abandon its nuclear weapons programs.

Some regional institutions have already been established,[4] including the Association of Southeast Asian Nations (ASEAN), ASEAN+3 (the ten members of the ASEAN plus China, Japan, and South Korea) and the East Asia Summit (EAS). Such institutions will be critical to resolving conflicts and establishing a framework for peace that can support regional prosperity and global leadership.

But that is only the first step. And whether Asian leaders share a common vision for regional integration remains unclear. Judging by Europe's experience — from the creation of the European Coal and Steel Community in 1951 to the establishment of the European Union in 1993 — there is no need to rush the integration process. But it will take a lot of time and effort.

Perhaps the best way to kick-start this process is to identify areas where the region can gain the most from integration, and take steps that will bring quick returns. For example, Asian countries can move toward a single market with common rules governing trade and free movement of workers, especially skilled ones. Launching the Regional Comprehensive Economic Partnership, a free-trade agreement currently being negotiated by ASEAN and six partners (Australia, China, India, Japan, South Korea, and New Zealand), would be an important step in this direction.

Given the vulnerability of cross-border capital flows, Asia must also pursue joint action on financial supervision, surveillance, and regulatory issues to prevent and manage crises. One specific goal should be to improve the Chiang Mai Initiative Multilateralization, a $240 billion currency-swap arrangement, and its surveillance unit, the ASEAN+3 Macroeconomic Research Office. Another should be to establish a *de facto* Asian Monetary Fund with a broader membership.

It should be noted that none of these efforts would aim to supplant existing sub-regional, regional, and global institutions. Rather, by making Asia a more effective and united actor, new regional trade and financial measures would complement and strengthen current arrangements.

For any of this to work, bureaucracies and the private sector, including business leaders and academics, must actively support high-level political commitments to integration. Such support should not be too difficult to muster. After all, integration would facilitate the exchange of valuable knowledge, from effective economic and social policies to technological and scientific insight.

Forums and dialogues on regional public goods could also prove valuable by promoting cooperation on cross-border challenges, including epidemics, natural disasters, and environmental degradation. Person-to-person connections would help to highlight for Asian societies their cultural commonalities and shared values, fostering progress in areas where particular countries might lag.

At a time when the global order is increasingly uncertain, Asia should take its fate into its own hands, by pursuing closer economic and political regional cooperation. If Asian countries can develop a shared vision for an economic community and a political association, this century could be theirs.

The Sino-Korean Trade War Must End*

Source: Zerbor / Shutterstock.com.

* Originally published in *Project Syndicate*, March 22, 2017.

S outh Korea has decided to deploy a US missile-defense system, and China is furious. Chinese leaders worry that the Terminal High Altitude Area Defense (THAAD) system will undermine its security and disrupt the regional strategic balance, by monitoring flights and missile launches in Chinese territory. But, as long as North Korea poses such an acute threat on the Korean Peninsula, China's opposition to it is pointless — and highly destructive.

As the United States and South Korea rush to deploy THAAD before the South's snap presidential election on May 9, China is ramping up economic sanctions, in the hope of compelling the next president to reconsider. Already, South Korea's tourism, consumer goods, and entertainment industries have been hit hard.

Chinese travel agencies have suspended the sale of group tours to South Korea. And China has temporarily closed the 55 discount stores owned by the Lotte Group — South Korea's fifth-largest conglomerate and the supplier of the land for the THAAD system — for supposed safety violations. Chinese media have issued[1] threats that sanctions could be extended to other South Korean companies, like Samsung and Hyundai.

China is eager to take advantage of its position as South Korea's largest trading partner, accounting for nearly one-quarter of its external trade, and main source of foreign tourism. (Chinese tourists accounted for half the total number of foreign visitors to South Korea last year — more than eight million people.)

But it is hardly a one-sided relationship. South Korea is China's fourth-largest trading partner, providing key intermediate inputs on which many Chinese firms rely. Indeed, intermediate and capital goods comprised[2] more than 70% of South Korea's exports to China last year, including key inputs such as semiconductors (20%) and display panels (11%). South Korea is also the number one source[3] of foreign tourists to China.

Given these dynamics, if the dispute over the THAAD system escalates into a full-fledged trade war, both China and South Korea will suffer. As we have seen in the recent past, protracted tensions — for example, the territorial disputes between China and Japan over the Senkaku/Diaoyu Islands in 2012 — can severely damage economic and diplomatic relations. Already, South Korea is considering bringing the Chinese sanctions to the World Trade Organization (WTO) for adjudication, and the authorities are reviewing whether China has violated relevant clauses of the two countries' bilateral free-trade agreement.

China and South Korea should protect the diplomatic relationship that they have maintained since 1992. But that requires China to recognize that South Korea's next president is unlikely to cancel the THAAD deployment, given the threat North Korea poses. If China continues to apply pressure for a concession on THAAD, the only result will be an increase in anti-Chinese sentiment in South Korea.

The good news is that the Chinese authorities seem to recognize these risks, the clearest sign being their apparent containment of anti-South Korea protests. China's leaders know that realizing their global leadership ambitions requires them to adhere to global norms and accept greater responsibility. In this context, South Korea's move to involve the WTO — and the risk to China's international reputation that a formal dispute would imply — may have focused Chinese leaders' minds concerning the risks of escalation.

This is not to say that the THAAD system's deployment is inevitable. If China devoted its energy to reining in its North Korean client, the threat confronting South Korea — and thus the South's need for an advanced missile shield — might be mitigated.

And yet some in China equate South Korea's THAAD deployment with North Korea's weapons programs. A recent article[4] in the *Global Times,* a nationalistic Chinese state paper, asserted that, if South Korea installs the THAAD system, it should face Chinese sanctions equivalent to those that are already choking North Korea.

This view fails to account for differences in intent. The North Korean regime, led by Kim Jong-un, is engaged in a remorseless quest to develop nuclear weapons and intercontinental missiles capable of delivering them. South Korea's leaders have agreed to deploy the THAAD system as a defensive maneuver.

Instead of imposing sanctions on South Korea, China should increase economic pressure on North Korea, say, by cutting off oil supplies. But economic sanctions alone aren't enough: the Kim regime has so far proved largely impervious to them. Given this, China would also need to engage with the US in sustained diplomatic efforts to reach a consensus on how to stabilize the Korean Peninsula and eliminate the risk of a military conflict.

Locked between China and Japan, the Korean Peninsula is, to use an old Korean saying, "a shrimp among whales," and it has been subjected to untold horrors as a result. The Korean War turned it into a proxy battleground for major powers, causing it to lose two million inhabitants in just three years. For nearly 70 years since then, the peninsula has been divided, and now it may be the world's most dangerous flashpoint.[5] Another major military conflict — bringing millions more deaths and a surge in refugees — must be avoided.

Warren Buffet famously said, "Only when the tide goes out do you discover who's been swimming naked." If world powers continue to delay tackling the North Korea threat, they will soon be exposed. US President Donald Trump and Chinese President Xi Jinping, who will meet next month, must work together to reduce tension on the Korean Peninsula, before they are caught with their pants down.

Part 3

Business, Money, and Finance

The Irresistible Rise of the Renminbi*

Source: Project Syndicate.

* Originally published in *Project Syndicate*, May 20, 2015.

By the end of this year, the International Monetary Fund will decide whether the Chinese renminbi will join the euro, the Japanese yen, the British pound, and the US dollar in the basket of currencies that determines the value of its international reserve asset, the Special Drawing Right (SDR). China is pushing hard for the renminbi's inclusion. Should it be admitted?

The IMF created the SDR in 1969 to supplement existing reserve currencies,[1] thereby providing the global financial system with additional liquidity. As it stands, the SDR's role remains largely limited to IMF operations; its share in global financial markets and central banks' international reserves is negligible. Nonetheless, adding the renminbi to the SDR basket would be symbolically important, implying recognition of China's growing global stature. The renminbi is already a major currency for world trade and investment, and accounts for a growing share of international financial transactions and reserve holdings.

To qualify for inclusion, the Chinese government has eased its capital controls and liberalized its financial markets considerably. Inclusion in the SDR basket would require continuing this process, which, together with the renminbi's emergence as a globally investable currency, would benefit the entire world economy.

The IMF's largest shareholders — the United States, Europe, and Japan — should thus welcome the renminbi's addition to the SDR basket. Yet opinions on the matter have been divided, with the US, in particular, reluctant to welcome China into the fold.

This is all the more problematic given that the 2008 financial crisis laid bare the international reserve system's inadequacy when it comes to ensuring sufficient liquidity for emerging economies. Although emerging economies have since accumulated larger foreign-exchange reserves and strengthened financial supervision and regulation, they remain vulnerable to external shocks, especially from the US, the eurozone, and Japan. All three have lately employed expansionary monetary policies; and, as the US Federal Reserve normalizes its policy, emerging economies will be hit again by a sudden withdrawal of global liquidity.

This continued vulnerability reflects a collective failure to reform the global monetary system — an imperative that People's Bank of China (PBOC) Governor Zhou Xiaochuan highlighted in early 2009.[2] Per

Zhou's proposal, China has championed a transition to a multi-currency reserve system, in which the SDR and an internationalized renminbi would be used more widely, including in countries' currency reserves. But its attempt in 2010 to add its currency to the SDR basket failed, because the renminbi was not "freely usable."

Since then, China has implemented a series of reforms to increase the renminbi's usage in foreign trade and direct investment, as well as in cross-border financial investment. Fourteen renminbi-clearing banks have been established worldwide. Last year, the Shanghai-Hong Kong Stock Connect was launched to stimulate cross-border investment and capital-market development. And China has signed bilateral currency-swap agreements with 28 central banks, including the Central Bank of Brazil, the Bank of Canada, the European Central Bank, and the Bank of England.

This year, Chinese policymakers have signaled further financial liberalization by removing the domestic cap on banks' deposit rates, thereby giving overseas institutional investors easier access to capital markets. The PBOC is also likely to widen the currency's trading band and move toward a more flexible exchange-rate regime.

As a result of these efforts, the renminbi has emerged as the second most used currency in trade finance, overtaking the euro, and the fifth most used for international payments. Moreover, it is increasingly preferred in currency-market transactions and official foreign-exchange reserves.

Of course, China stands to gain much from the renminbi's emergence as an alternative international reserve currency, sharing in the "exorbitant privilege" that the US currently enjoys by virtue of the dollar's global status. Beyond the convenience of conducting international transactions in local currency, China would be able to take advantage of seigniorage — safe in the knowledge that it would not face a balance-of-payments crisis.

But, in order to reach that point, China must confront significant risks. Capital-account liberalization and renminbi internationalization invite potentially volatile cross-border capital flows, which could, for example, trigger rapid currency appreciation. Given this, China can be expected to continue to manage capital-account transactions to some extent, using macroprudential measures and, when appropriate, direct capital controls.

Even if China manages to mitigate such risks, unseating the US dollar[3] as the dominant global currency will be no easy feat. Inertia favors currencies that are already in use internationally, and China lacks deep and liquid financial markets, an important precondition that any international reserve currency must meet. Furthermore, China's banking system, which remains subject to extensive government control, lags far behind those of the US and Europe in terms of efficiency and transparency.

If, however, China succeeds in developing a more convertible capital account and bolstering its financial system's efficiency, the renminbi is likely to emerge as a new international reserve currency, complementing the US dollar and the euro. This would benefit companies and central banks alike, by enabling them to diversify their foreign-currency holdings further.

History suggests that a shift in global currency dominance is likely to occur gradually. For now, China is focused on winning the renminbi's inclusion, even with a small share, in the SDR currency basket. The IMF's major shareholders should seriously consider it. The renminbi's continued internationalization, not to mention further progress on critical financial reforms, would contribute to the creation of a more stable and efficient global reserve system.

Asia's View of the Greek Crisis*

Source: anyaivanova / Shutterstock.com.

---

*Originally published in *Project Syndicate*, July 16, 2015.

A sian countries have been watching the Greek crisis unfold with a mixture of envy and schadenfreude. When they experienced their own financial crisis in 1997, they received far less aid, with far harsher conditions. But they also recovered much more strongly, suggesting that ever-growing bailouts may not be the best prescription for recovery.

Since the onset of the crisis, Greece has received massive financing from the so-called "troika": the European Commission, the European Central Bank, and the International Monetary Fund. It received bailout packages in 2010 and 2012 totaling €240 billion ($266 billion), including €30 billion from the IMF, more than triple Greece's cumulative limit for IMF borrowing. The latest deal promises up to another €86 billion.

By contrast, South Korea's 1997 bailout package — which was larger than those received by Indonesia, Thailand, or the Philippines — totaled $57 billion, with $21 billion coming from the IMF. At the time, South Korea's annual GDP was $560 billion; in 2014, Greek GDP amounted to less than $240 billion.[1]

The IMF seems to have lent Greece such a large amount for political reasons. For starters, at the onset of the crisis, then-IMF Managing Director Dominique Strauss-Kahn was a leading candidate to become President of France. More generally, major IMF shareholders, the European Union, and the United States have a vital interest in stabilizing Greece to safeguard French and German banks and preserve NATO unity. Desmon Lachman, a former deputy director of the IMF's policy department, has called the institution a slush fund,[2] abused by its political masters during the Greek crisis.

To be sure, the economic mess created in Greece — the result of government profligacy, official corruption, and widespread tax evasion — merited some international assistance. And the IMF did impose conditions on its loans to Greece — including fiscal austerity, privatization, and structural reform of its pension and tax systems — most of which were necessary to address the country's insolvency. The requirements of the latest rescue deal are the toughest yet — even tougher than those that Greek voters overwhelmingly rejected in a referendum earlier this month.

But the scale of the aid remains massive, especially when one considers how little progress Greece has made in implementing the reforms it promised in the past. This contrasts sharply with Asia's experience in 1997.

Unlike Greece, Asia's problem was not an insolvency crisis, but a liquidity crisis, caused by a sudden reversal[3] of capital flows. In South Korea, net private-capital inflows of 4.8% of GDP in 1996 swung to net outflows of 3.4% of GDP in 1997. Though the accumulation of substantial short-term debts in the financial system and corporate sector did amplify the shocks, the primary factors fueling the crisis were the lack of international liquidity, panicked behavior by investors, and financial contagion.

Yet the IMF imposed even tougher conditions[4] on Asia than it has on Greece, including fiscal austerity, monetary tightening, and financial restructuring. Some of these requirements were clearly unnecessary, as evidenced by Malaysia, which recovered quickly from the crisis without IMF assistance.

In any case, the actions were temporary. Once confidence began to recover and market conditions stabilized, the East Asian economies shifted their monetary and fiscal policies toward expansion and embraced large-scale exchange-rate depreciation — efforts that enhanced their export competitiveness.[5] Structural reforms, including the immediate closing of financial institutions and the elimination of non-performing loans, also helped to bolster recovery.

In South Korea, for example, real GDP growth quickly rebounded from -6.7% in 1998 to 9.5% in 1999. By mid-2003, some 776 of the country's financial institutions were closed. And the authorities' strong commitment to reform restored investor confidence, reviving inflows of private capital and reactivating foreign trade.

Greece, by contrast, has utterly failed to engineer a recovery. Instead of dropping to 110% as planned, the public debt-to-GDP ratio has increased to 170%. Annual *per capita* real income contracted 4.8%, on average, over the last six years. Unemployment stands at 26%, and hovers around 50% among young people.

Against this background, it was not shocking that Greece, unable to come up with €1.5 billion at the end of June, became the first developed country to miss a payment to the IMF. Belatedly, the Fund acknowledged[6] that its lending and policy advice had failed in Greece.

Greece's government then demanded more financial support with less stringent conditions. But, as its creditors have now recognized, providing more money will not address Greece's insolvency. That is why the new deal requires that the government immediately cut pensions, hike taxes (beginning with the value-added tax), liberalize the labor market, and adhere to severe spending constraints. At the same time, a write-down of official debt, like the "haircut" given to private creditors in 2012, will be necessary.

Many have questioned whether agonizing reforms are entirely necessary; if the country returned to the *drachma*, they suggest, it could implement interest-rate cuts and devalue its exchange rate, thereby engineering an export-led recovery. But, given Greece's small export sector, not to mention the weakness of the global economy, such a recovery may be impossible. Greece's best bet is reform.

So far, Greece has shown itself to be unwilling to implement a painful internal-wage adjustment and reform measures forced by outsiders. Perhaps the latest deal, which was reached with Greece on the brink, will prove to be a turning point, with Greece finally committing actively to economic and fiscal reform. Otherwise, Greece's exit from the eurozone — with all the concomitant social and economic strife — seems all but inevitable.

Asians watch with sympathy the fall from grace of the birthplace of Western civilization. But perhaps Greece should look to Asia for proof that, by taking responsibility for its own destiny, a country can emerge stronger from even the most difficult trials.

Closing Asia's Emerging Skills Gap*

Source: Project Syndicate.

---

*Originally published in *Project Syndicate*, January 14, 2016.

A sia is facing a human-capital challenge. Over the last three decades, significant gains in workforce size and quality helped Asia to become a hub of global supply chains — and thus to sustain rapid progress toward advanced-economy income levels and living standards. But with workers increasingly unable to meet the demands of the labor market, the region's remarkable development success could be derailed.

Asia has plenty of educated young workers. But, at a time of industrial upgrading and ever-increasing technological sophistication, the knowledge and skills gained in school are often insufficient. As a result, youth unemployment, underemployment, and job dissatisfaction are on the rise.

Throughout Asia, a significant share of workers feel they are over- or under-educated for their jobs, while employers often lament a lack of qualified graduates. A Manpower Group survey shows that 48% of employers[1] had difficulty filling vacancies in Asia in 2015, compared to 28% in 2006. Meanwhile, many university graduates — including a whopping 45% in South Korea[2] — are struggling to find jobs.

Despite variations among countries in Asia, some weaknesses in policies and systems designed to boost skills development are endemic. Among the most damaging is the inability of many countries to impart the right skills through pre-employment and on-the-job training.

In India, for example, only 0.8% of students,[3] on average, participated in formal technical and vocational education at the secondary level from 2006 to 2010. The country's technical and vocational education and training (TVET) system has enough capacity to train less than one-quarter of the 13 million people[4] entering the labor market each year. TVET is rarely available to workers in small and medium-size enterprises (SMEs) or the informal sector, and it receives too little public financing.

Moreover, across Asia, a lack of involvement by private companies — that is, potential employers — further undermines the ability of TVET systems to respond adequately to changes in the labor market, thereby reducing graduate employability. In Bangladesh, Indonesia, and Sri Lanka, less than one-quarter of companies[5] conduct formal in-house training. A dearth of well-qualified teachers and ineffective governance exacerbates the situation.

Governments across Asia must devise ways to transform their education and training systems, so that workers acquire the skills they need to boost economic growth and productivity — the key to better jobs and higher wages. Most important, governments must make skills acquisition a central feature of national development policies. At a time of rapid change, education and skills training should be coordinated with, say, trade and industrial policies to improve the chances that emerging labor-market requirements will be met.

Moreover, general education and TVET systems need to be restructured. In many Asian countries, formal education is often overly academic or simply low-quality, undermining not only graduates' employability, but also their capacity to reap the benefits of further TVET. To be effective, secondary and tertiary schools must produce graduates with both soft skills, such as communication and teamwork, and relevant technical skills. Here, stronger partnerships between educators and employers to develop curriculum standards, create internship opportunities, and provide financing would be help significantly.

As for TVET systems, both their capacity and quality must be improved. As governments improve their capacity for supervision, coordination, and regulation of the TVET system, actual skills training should be shifted to the private sector, thereby transforming the current supply-driven system to one that responds effectively to changing market demand.

To this end, governments should encourage public-private partnerships focused on, for example, identifying the labor market's unmet needs, setting TVET policy priorities, developing curricula and national standards, training TVET teachers, and implementing cost-sharing mechanisms. Governments must also ensure better access to TVET systems for disadvantaged groups, including children from poor families and rural areas and employees in SMEs and the informal sector.

Given that the challenge of upgrading educational and skills-training systems is shared across Asia, national governments should not be working in isolation. More knowledge-sharing, especially with regard to curriculum development and teacher training, as well as expert and student exchanges and improved technology-sharing, would strengthen everyone's efforts considerably. Moreover, promoting greater student/worker mobility and improving labor-market flexibility, both within countries and across the region, would help to improve the allocation of skilled workers.

In the coming decades, Asia will continue to contribute a large number of workers to the global labor market. How well equipped these workers are to meet ever-evolving market needs will be a key factor influencing not only Asia's trajectory, but also that of the entire global economy.

The Way Back for Monetary Policy*

Source: Pablo Prat / Shutterstock.com.

*Originally published in *Project Syndicate*, May 17, 2016.

The central banks of major advanced economies have been navigating uncharted territory in recent years. While their use of a range of unconventional monetary-policy tools has had benefits, it has also generated significant uncertainty, without fully stabilizing the world economy. Now the time has come to head back toward more familiar policy terrain.

Following the 2008 financial meltdown, the US Federal Reserve cut the policy rate to almost zero and pursued so-called quantitative easing (QE), by purchasing long-term securities from the public and private sectors. The central banks of the European Union, Japan, and the United Kingdom soon launched similar unconventional programs. The result was a vast amount of cheap liquidity that helped to stabilize the financial sector, restore stock and real-estate prices, and increase domestic demand. All of this helped to limit the fallout of the financial crisis and push the global economy toward recovery.

But this aggressive approach has its limits. Indeed, as Reserve Bank of India Governor Raghuram Rajan[1] has pointed out,[2] after years of effort, the benefits of unconventional monetary policy are diminishing, while the costs are increasing. Recognizing this, the Fed ended QE at the end of last year and raised its policy rate by 25 basis points. The rate hikes will likely continue this year, though the speed and extent of the increases are uncertain.

Yet the European Central Bank and the Bank of Japan (BOJ) have decided to sustain their QE programs. Moreover, they have adopted a negative interest-rate policy — which amounts to charging a fee for bank reserves — to revitalize depressed demand. Unsurprisingly, the effects on inflation and real output have been limited.

Monetary policy is an effective means of managing inflation and can boost employment and output in a recession. Lowering interest rates below zero, however, has hurt banks' balance sheets, reducing their lending capacity. As a result, it has failed[3] to increase business investment. Even low positive interest rates, if maintained for a prolonged period, could backfire, fueling asset bubbles and enabling household and corporate debt to grow to unsustainable levels.

Meanwhile, asset purchases have caused the balance sheets of major central banks to swell to unprecedented levels. The orderly rewinding that is now needed will be very difficult to manage.

Beyond the domestic sphere, unconventional monetary policies have had far-reaching spillover effects. In particular, they have sent emerging economies, with their financial links to advanced economies, on a capital-flow roller-coaster ride.

First, the emerging economies were flooded with liquidity flowing from the advanced economies. Large capital inflows led to overheating and inflation, asset-price bubbles, and rapid currency appreciation. Then, the Fed's tapering of QE led to the sudden withdrawal of that capital, creating a risk of financial disruption and currency crises. The emerging economies' monetary authorities have struggled to cope with these shocks using available instruments, including interest rates, exchange rates, prudential regulation, and capital controls.

But that is not all. Because advanced economies' unconventional monetary policies have also depreciated their currencies and stimulated their exports, the risk of competitive devaluations is now a real concern. If, say, the BOJ moved to intervene outright in the exchange-rate markets to depreciate the yen, the odds that the People's Bank of China and the Bank of Korea would opt for weaker currencies would increase. All of this would be highly destabilizing, particularly for emerging economies like Brazil that are facing a brutal combination of internal and external challenges.

Instead of viewing all of this as motivation to back away from unconventional monetary policy, however, some economists are recommending that the ECB and the BOJ pursue an even more extraordinary policy: so-called "helicopter drops." The idea, introduced by the Nobel laureate economist Milton Friedman in 1969, entails the distribution of freshly printed money directly to the public, with a commitment from the central bank never to withdraw it. As Former Fed Chairman Ben Bernanke points out,[4] monetary finance is essentially equivalent to a broad-based tax cut, with the central bank committing to purchase government debt.

Among the influential economists advocating helicopter drops for Europe and Japan are Bernanke, Willem Buiter,[5] Kemal Derviş,[6] and Adair Turner.[7] They argue that even if it is not an ideal solution, it can cure their economies. For governments restrained by high public debt and deficits, the proposal is certainly tempting.

But helicopter drops are highly risky. As Bernanke himself warns,[8] such a policy could undermine central banks' long-term independence.

Moreover, it would enable governments to monetize fiscal deficits without constraints, and potentially to abuse money-printing power for political considerations. And it might not even work as intended, with the money benefiting only certain groups. Given the difficulty of regaining lost sovereignty and credibility, central banks must keep helicopter drops as a last resort.

The reality is that recourse to easy windfalls produced through loose monetary policy could have serious long-term repercussions, especially if they are used to delay efforts to address underlying issues. Japanese Prime Minister Shinzo Abe's economic revitalization strategy — so-called Abenomics — is a case in point. The strategy was supposed to use a mix of monetary and fiscal expansion to help facilitate structural reforms. Yet the reforms have faced delays, and employment and output growth has been limited.

What advanced-country central banks should be doing now is implementing monetary policies aimed at restoring their credibility, while governments focus on implementing effective fiscal policies and structural reforms. Crucially, advanced and emerging economies must coordinate their policies, in order to foster confidence and strengthen growth. This is the only way back onto the path of sustained global economic health.

Last month, finance ministers and central-bank governors of the G-20 countries acknowledged the limitations of monetary stimulus and embraced[9] structural reforms, infrastructure investment, and fiscal policy as the key to future growth. But they have yet to back their words with strong action. Their credibility — not to mention the fate of the global economy — is on the line.

Taming the Chaebols*

Source: Sagase48 / Shutterstock.com.

*Originally published in *Project Syndicate*, January 19, 2017.

The indictment of Lee Jae-yong, the heir apparent at Samsung, is but the latest explosive development in the political scandal that has been rocking South Korea. Already, the National Assembly voted to impeach President Park Geun-hye, the daughter of former president Park Chung-hee, on December 9. The Constitutional Court now has six months to justify her permanent removal from office. Depending on its decision, a presidential election may be held in the next few months.

But, as Lee's indictment demonstrates, more than the presidency is at stake in this crisis. At the heart of the scandal is the reciprocal relationship between politicians and the chaebols, South Korea's giant family-owned conglomerates. If the government takes this opportunity to transform the economy's chaebol-dominated structure, it would reshape the country's economic future as well — for the better.

Park is accused of using her political influence to benefit her longtime confidante, Choi Soon-sil, who is charged with forcing the chaebols to funnel about 80 billion Korean won ($70 million) into two nonprofit cultural foundations that she effectively controlled. She is also suspected of interfering in various state affairs, including ministerial appointments and state visits, despite having no official position. Park is being ridiculed[1] as Choi's puppet.

To some extent, this is nothing new in South Korea. Most administrations have extracted money from the chaebols, often with the help of prosecutors and the tax authorities. In exchange for that money, which is used to finance costly state projects or even political campaigns, the chaebols gain favors, such as cheap bank loans or preferential regulations.

This reciprocal relationship has existed since the start of South Korea's economic transformation in the 1960s. The country's rapid progress is attributed to strong manufacturing exports, carried out by firms that were able to compete in global markets only with the help of government incentives.

Park's father, who led South Korea from 1961 until his assassination in 1979, worked closely with the chaebols, helping them first to build comparative advantages in labor-intensive manufacturing and then to progress to more capital-intensive industries, including automobiles, shipbuilding, and chemicals.

Today, the chaebols produce almost two-thirds of South Korea's exports — no small feat, in the world's sixth-largest exporting country. Samsung Electronics is the largest chaebol, and accounts for 20% of total exports. Ranking 13th on the Fortune 2016 Global 500,[2] Samsung's market capitalization comprises one-fifth of the South Korean stock market.

Beyond government support, the chaebols' ownership and governance structure has contributed to their success. With the founding families in charge, chaebols' top management can focus on a long-term vision, instead of short-term profits, and can mobilize resources swiftly. The efficiency of this model is apparent in the chaebols' success as "fast followers" of top US and Japanese firms.

Yet the chaebols' hierarchical management structure is often too rigid to correct bad decisions. Many conglomerates went bankrupt during the 1997 Asian financial crisis, having made excessive and unprofitable investments.

Moreover, the chaebols' ownership is often opaque, with webs of cross-shareholdings allowing founding families to exercise controlling power, despite holding only a small portion of equity. The Lee family has less than 5% direct ownership of Samsung Electronics, but holds a 31.1% stake in Samsung C&T, the group's *de facto* holding company, which owns a 4.3% stake in Samsung Electronics and a 19.3% stake in Samsung Life Insurance. Samsung Life Insurance, in turn, has a 7.3% stake in Samsung Electronics, which indirectly invests in Samsung C&T and Samsung Life Insurance.

This type of ownership structure can be particularly problematic during transfers of ownership to new generations. As with any dynasty, no one is ever sure that the heir apparent is capable of doing the job. Lee recently took over as Samsung Electronics' vice chairman. At a time of strong and growing market competition, he must provide the kind of visionary leadership that characterized his father and grandfather, the company's pioneering founder, who transformed a small local trading company into a global semiconductor and smartphone powerhouse.

Like the rest of the chaebols, Samsung risks losing ground in global markets, owing to the narrowing technology gap with China. Though South Korea is still ahead of China in high-tech branches like memory chips and automobiles, its lead is diminishing in many major industries, such as steel, ships, petrochemicals, and electronics. In emerging markets, Samsung Electronics has already lost market share to Chinese smartphone makers such as Huawei and OPPO.

It is in this high-pressure context that, last year, Moon Hyung-pyo, South Korea's then-health and welfare minister, allegedly pressured the National Pension Service to back a controversial merger of two Samsung group affiliates that was essential to ensure a smooth transfer of managerial control to Lee. Moon, who then became chair of the NPS, has now been arrested for that move.

Lee's indictment, too, is linked to this effort. He is charged with donating to Choi's two foundations, and of bankrolling Choi's daughter, in exchange for the support he received. He is also accused of embezzlement and perjury. (The judge ruled that there was insufficient reason to issue the requested arrest warrant.)

While the government makes deals with the chaebols, start-ups and small and medium-size enterprises (SMEs) are struggling to make their way into the market. SMEs' labor productivity[3] is just 35% that of large firms. And labor productivity[4] in the services sector is 45% that of the manufacturing sector — just half the OECD average.

To create a healthier business climate for innovative small firms and venture startups, the chaebols' dominance must end. South Korea's leaders must implement stronger regulations to prevent illegal transactions and unfair practices, including collusion between chaebols and government officials. They should also strengthen the rights of minority shareholders and outside directors to prevent expropriation by founding families.

There was a time when what was good for the chaebols was good for South Korea. But times have changed, and the chaebol system is now doing more harm than good. With Park's impeachment, South Korea has gained an ideal opportunity to leave behind her father's legacy as well.

Part 4
Education and Society

South Korea's Feminine Future*

Source: MIND AND I / Shutterstock.com.

*Originally published in *Project Syndicate*, March 20, 2014.

Over the last half-century, South Korea has made considerable economic progress, with *per capita income*[1] increasing from a mere $80 dollars in 1960 to more than $22,000 last year. But its potential for sustained growth is faltering, owing to the imminent decline of its working-age population[2] — projected to fall by 25% by 2050 — and rising competition from China and other emerging economies. In order to improve its prospects, South Korea must pursue economic reform and restructuring, with an emphasis on maximizing its human-capital resources — especially women.

South Korea's success over the last five decades owes much to the rapid growth of its well-educated labor force. From 1960 to 2010, the share of adults with a secondary education soared from 20% to an impressive 87%. By boosting productivity, increasing returns on investment, and facilitating technological adaption and innovation, South Korea's abundance of well-educated workers has served as the foundation for its export-oriented development strategy.

But women remain underutilized, to the detriment of the entire economy. Indeed, any effective South Korean growth strategy must create more and better economic opportunities for women, in part by establishing more accommodating working environments and instituting a more diverse and flexible education system.

To its credit, South Korea has built a relatively gender-equal society. The gender gap in enrollment in both secondary and higher education is very small; and women's access to elite positions in law, medicine, and the civil service has increased considerably in recent years. The country elected its first female president, Park Geun-hye, in 2012.

But a significant gender gap remains in terms of the return on human capital. According to OECD data,[3] only 55% of South Korean women aged 15–64 are in the labor force, compared to an average of 65% in the advanced economies. South Korea's male labor-force participation rate, by contrast, stands at about 77% — close to the OECD average of 79%.

Women who have completed secondary or tertiary education are more likely to enter and remain in the labor market than their less educated counterparts. The labor-participation rate for women with post-secondary education is 64%, far exceeding the 35% rate for those with only a primary or middle-school education.

But, even for South Korea's most highly educated and capable female workers, child rearing is a major career obstacle. In fact, South Korean women participate in the labor force at roughly the average rate for the OECD while they are in their late twenties. The problem is that the rate drops sharply from 71% to 57% among women in their 30's, as inflexible working environments and a lack of affordable childcare undermine their ability to continue investing in their careers.

The good news is that Park's government is working to change this. Indeed, its three-year plan for economic innovation,[4] announced in February, aims to raise the female employment rate to 62% by 2017, through the provision of affordable, high-quality childcare facilities and expanded paid parental leave, among other measures.

But it is less clear how the government will create additional jobs for women. It could, for example, split full-time jobs into multiple part-time positions, and offer incentives for workers to reduce their hours. But, given that South Korea's workforce already includes a substantial share of non-regular workers,[5] increasing temporary employment may not contribute to economic growth.

A better approach would entail creating high-quality jobs in modern service industries. As it stands, while the services sector accounts for more than 70% of employment[6] in South Korea, its productivity-growth rate remains much lower than that of the manufacturing sector. Too many people are working in traditional, low-productivity service industries, such as wholesale, retail trade, and restaurants, leaving modern, high-productivity services like communications, health, financial intermediation, and business services underdeveloped.

It is also important to narrow the mismatch between women's abilities and their career paths. The current system tends to reinforce gender roles, encouraging children to follow culturally framed paths, instead of nurturing their individual interests and potential.

For example, female university students are much more likely to study humanities than the so-called "STEM" subjects (science, technology, engineering, and mathematics) — key drivers of productivity gains, innovation, and economic growth. Efforts by primary and secondary schools could help to foster more diverse interests among female students, giving talented young women the tools they need to make important contributions to key economic sectors.

Of course, the potential of educated, empowered women to drive sustained economic growth is not limited to South Korea. Japanese Prime Minister Shinzo Abe, too, has identified[7] increased female labor-force participation as critical to efforts to revive his country's long-dormant economy.

In South Korea, Japan, and elsewhere, developing and maximizing women's potential will require comprehensive education and labor-market reforms, as well as structural change, particularly on the services side of the economy. The question is whether political leaders are ready to back their lofty pronouncements with decisive action.

China's Education Revolution*

Source: humphery / Shutterstock.com.

* Originally published in *Project Syndicate*, May 20, 2014.

Over the last 35 years, China's strong and sustained output growth — averaging more than 9.5% annually — has driven the miraculous transformation of a rural, command economy into a global economic superpower. In fact, according to the World Bank's most recent calculation[1] of the purchasing power of aggregate income, China is about to overtake the United States as the world's largest economy. But, in terms of the quality and sustainability of its growth model, China still has a long way to go.

Despite its remarkable rise, China's *per capita* income, at $10,057 (adjusted for purchasing power) in 2011, ranks 99th in the world — roughly one-fifth of US *per capita* income of $49,782. And reaching high-income status is no easy feat. Indeed, many countries have tried and failed, leaving them in a so-called middle-income trap,[2] in which *per capita* income levels stagnate before crossing the high-income threshold.

Strong human capital is critical to enable China to escape this fate. But China's labor force currently lacks the skills needed to support high-tech, high-value industries. Changing this will require comprehensive education reform that expands and improves opportunities for children, while strengthening skills training for adults.

To be sure, over the last four decades, the quality of China's labor force has improved substantially, which is reflected in impressive gains in educational attainment. Gross enrollment rates at the primary level have surpassed 100% since the 1990's, while secondary and tertiary enrollment rates reached 87% and 24%, respectively, in 2012. In 2010, more than 70% of Chinese citizens[3] aged 15–64 had received secondary education, compared to about 20% in 1970.

Furthermore, Chinese students perform well in internationally comparable tests. Fifteen-year-olds in Shanghai outperformed students from 65 countries, including 34 OECD countries, in mathematics, science, and reading, according to the Program for International Student Assessment in 2009[4] and 2012.[5]

China has also benefited from rapid employment growth, with more than seven million workers having entered the workforce each year since 1990. This, together with the massive reallocation of workers from rural to urban areas, has supported the labor-intensive manufacturing industries that have fueled China's economic rise.

But China's demographic advantage is diminishing quickly, owing to low fertility rates and population aging. According to the United Nations, by 2030, China's working-age population (15–59 years old) will have decreased by 67 million[6] from its 2010 level.

Moreover, higher education in China leaves much to be desired, with employer surveys revealing that graduates of upper secondary schools and universities usually lack the required technical knowledge and soft skills. For example, in 2013, more than one-third of the Chinese firms surveyed[7] said that they struggled to recruit skilled workers, with 61% attributing this to a shortage of general employable skills. How, then, can China expect to achieve the export diversification and technological upgrading that it needs to move up the global value chain?

Clearly, China needs to reform its higher-education institutions, including technical and vocational training programs. At the same time, it must expand opportunities for anyone with talent to acquire high-quality secondary and tertiary education, thereby reducing substantial disparities in the accessibility and quality of higher education across regions and social groups. And the children of migrant workers in urban areas must be granted full access to the education system. Such efforts to reduce educational disparities would help to address income inequality — a significant threat to China's future economic growth.

All of this will require increased public investment in education. As it stands, China's public investment in education, as a share of GDP, is below international standards[8] across all levels, but especially in senior secondary and tertiary education.

China's education challenge also extends to quality. Inadequate education is a major driver of rising unemployment among China's senior secondary and tertiary graduates, not to mention their declining wage premium. This can be remedied through better financing, more effective recruitment and compensation policies, and more decentralized decision-making in school administrations.

Finally, though some evidence suggests that there is an over-supply of university graduates in China, ongoing demographic and sectoral shifts mean that China will encounter a supply deficit[9] of 24 million highly skilled graduates of universities or higher-level vocational schools by 2020. To fill this gap, China must upgrade its fragmented and ineffective technical- and vocational-training programs.

To ensure that its labor force can meet the demands of a rapidly changing economic and technological environment, China must build a more inclusive, higher quality education system. Without it, China may not be the world's number one economy for long.

Education and Opportunity*

Source: Amlan Mathur / Shutterstock.com.

*Originally published in *Project Syndicate*, September 11, 2014.

Education is a fundamental driver of personal, national, and global development. Since the beginning of the century, recognition of this has driven many countries to pursue the Millennium Development Goal[1] of achieving universal primary education and eradicating gender disparities at all levels of education by 2015. This has contributed to considerable progress in expanding educational opportunities and attainment worldwide. But there is much more to be done.

To be sure, universal primary education has nearly been achieved. Moreover, considerable progress has been made toward gender equality in educational opportunities and attainment. Indeed, enrollment rates for school-age females have increased steadily at all levels, reaching near parity with male enrollment globally. As a result, the gender gap in average years of schooling for the adult population — a widely used measure of educational attainment — has narrowed.

Moreover, in 2010, for people aged 25 and above, the female-to-male ratio in average years of schooling[2] was almost 100% in advanced countries and about 85% in developing regions. But, in many low-income countries in Sub-Saharan Africa, the Middle East, and South Asia, girls still have far less access to education, especially at the secondary and tertiary levels, than boys do.

Significant global disparities also remain in post-primary education and the quality of schooling. In advanced countries, almost 90% of the population[3] aged 15–64 has attained at least some secondary education, compared to only 63% in developing countries. Likewise, though more than 33% of the working-age population in advanced countries has achieved some level of tertiary education, the proportion is just 12% in the developing world.

Academic research[4] suggests that countries with higher *per capita* income, lower income inequality, and lower fertility rates tend to invest more in children's education, with public expenditure leading to higher enrollment rates. The logical conclusion is that efforts to promote more inclusive economic growth and improve education systems can raise enrollment among young people in developing countries and reduce disparities between genders and among social groups.

But simply narrowing the gaps in school-enrollment rates and total years of schooling is not enough. Countries must also ensure the quality of their education systems — a key challenge for the coming decades.

As it stands, poor educational outcomes and inefficient education systems are eliciting deep concern worldwide. In many countries, primary schools fail to provide students with appropriate cognitive skills like numeracy, literacy, problem-solving ability, and general scientific knowledge.

Furthermore, inadequate education at the secondary and tertiary levels, including technical and vocational education and training, is leaving students unequipped to meet the job market's changing demands. As a result, many countries are struggling with a mismatch between the skills that employers seek and those that workers have.

Wide disparities in educational quality, often measured by student achievement on international examinations, are evident within and across countries. The results of most internationally comparable mathematics, reading, and science exams for primary and secondary students reveal a considerable gap not only between advanced and developing countries, but also across the developing world. According to the Trends in International Mathematics and Science Study,[5] South Korea had the highest average score (590) in 2011 on the science test for secondary students, while Ghana scored the lowest (306).

Though academic performance is determined largely by family inputs and students' individual talents, other factors, such as the amount of school resources available to students, also play an important role, as do various other school inputs, such as teacher quality, class size, expenditure per pupil, and instruction time.

The institutional features of education systems are another important determinant of student achievement. Private financing and provision, school autonomy, and external monitoring and assessment mechanisms tend to influence the quality of education[6] by changing the incentives for students and teachers.

In the future, new information and communication technologies are expected to stimulate the expansion of educational opportunities and to improve educational quality at the national and global level, by offering a variety of innovative learning channels. For example, the ability to use new technologies to build borderless networks among schools can offer opportunities for students in low-income countries to learn from teachers in advanced countries — and *vice versa*.

The imperative is clear. Global leaders must commit to enhancing the quality of education and reduce the education gap by increasing school resources, improving the efficiency of educational institutions, and seizing the opportunities afforded by technological innovation. All of this will serve to enrich human capital, which is essential to boosting productivity and incomes.

Indeed, if such efforts are designed specifically to ensure equal opportunities for all, regardless of gender or wealth, they will be a boon to the global economy, while promoting social cohesion at the national level. When it comes to improving education, there really is no downside.

Asia's Almighty Middle Class*

Source: LennonLand / Shutterstock.com.

---

*Originally published in *Project Syndicate*, March 19, 2015.

espite recent economic uncertainty, Asia's middle class is growing fast. In the coming decades, this burgeoning demographic
segment will serve as a keystone for economic and political
development in the region, with significant implications for the rest of
the world.

The OECD estimates[1] that the global middle class (defined as households with daily expenditures of $10–100 per person, in 2005 purchasing
power parity terms) will swell to 4.9 billion people by 2030, from 1.8 billion in 2009. Two-thirds are expected to reside in Asia, up from 28% in
2009, with China home to the largest share. Indeed, if China pursues the
structural reforms and technological upgrading needed to maintain rapid
economic growth, its middle class[2] should exceed one billion people in
2030, up from 157 million in 2009.

The rapid emergence of Asia's middle class will bring far-reaching
economic change, creating new market opportunities for domestic and
international companies. Already, demand for consumer durables has
increased in the region, with China becoming the world's largest market
for automobiles and mobile phones. But there remains substantial room
for more consumption in luxury goods and technological products, as the
purchasing power of the developing world's middle class catches up to
that in the advanced countries.

This convergence will contribute to more sustainable economic
growth, with Asia's economies rebalancing toward domestic demand,
especially household consumption, and thereby becoming less vulnerable
to external shocks. Given the decline in export demand since the global
economic crisis, this shift could not be timelier. And the benefits will not
be confined to Asia; as imports to the region increase, global trade imbalances will decline, improving the sustainability of economic growth
worldwide.

Indeed, Asia's growing middle class will transform a region known as
a global manufacturing hub into a consumption powerhouse. As demand
rises, more and better jobs will be created not only in Asia, but also globally, along supply chains and across production networks.

With rising prosperity comes improved education and health care,
which promise to help drive long-term economic growth by improving productivity. In China, this would represent a significant shift from prevailing

conditions, in which the children of poor households,[3] especially in rural areas, lag in terms of nutrition and school enrollment, despite significant progress in recent decades on lowering infant mortality and raising educational attainment.

Equipped with high-quality education, Asia's rising middle class will demand higher-quality public services. Increased confidence in their country's political systems and institutional structures, enhanced by improved perceptions of upward mobility, will help to strengthen the rule of law. And there will be more opportunities for women to learn and work, leading to greater gender equality.

Most important, the rise of the middle class is likely to be accompanied by growing demands for political freedom and civil liberties, thereby fostering democratization. Indeed, an examination of a large sample of countries,[4] from the nineteenth to the twenty-first centuries, reveals that a larger population of affluent, educated citizens — especially women — brings about more political participation and greater support for democracy, particularly in less-developed countries.

In the West, capitalism and democracy progressed in tandem, as the development of markets reduced the power of landlords and increased that of the working and middle classes. By participating actively in politics, basing their electoral choices on rational self-interest, and developing the sense of moderation needed to resist dictatorship, the middle class promotes democratic progress. At the same time, the growth of private organizations associated with the rise of the middle class prevents state institutions from monopolizing political resources.

In Asia, South Korea experienced a similar progression, with rapid economic growth spurring the rise of a large middle class, which in turn drove democratization in the 1980s. That history may repeat in China before long.

Given the benefits of having a large middle class, Asian countries should be nurturing theirs by improving health care, upgrading infrastructure, investing in universities and technical training, and addressing income and educational disparities. Moreover, social safety nets should be created or strengthened, in order to help safeguard the middle class from negative shocks and boost consumption growth (which continues to be hampered by precautionary saving).

Finally, public policies — aimed at strengthening the rule of law, promoting trade, and achieving sound macroeconomic management — are essential to sustain growth, thereby ensuring the continuous upward mobility of lower-income families. That upward mobility is the key to keeping in motion a virtuous circle of middle-class expansion and economic growth.

Can South Korea Make More Babies?*

---

*Originally published in *Project Syndicate*, September 23, 2016.

South Korea is facing major demographic challenges. The total fertility rate (the number of children per woman), at 1.24, is one of the lowest in the world, and well below the level — 2.1 children per woman — needed to sustain a population without immigration. As a result, the population is aging fast, and the government, despite its best efforts, seems to have no answer.

A low birthrate is common in industrialized countries. Before South Korea's economic boom — a time when having more children was viewed as a source of security in old age — the fertility rate was much higher,[1] averaging more than six until 1960. But, as South Korea's economy advanced, child-rearing costs rose, and female labor-force participation increased, the fertility rate declined dramatically, dropping below two in the 1980s.

At first, falling fertility rates were an economic blessing, as households saved more and invested in children's development. In 2015, the college enrollment rate for women hit[2] 81%, compared to just 6% in 1980. But the decline of the prime working-age population has lately been undercutting economic growth, and threatens to place excessive pressure on the public pension system down the road.

South Korea's government has attempted to address these challenges with a series of measures aimed at boosting fertility rates. A recent package includes more paternity leave, priority enrollment in public childcare facilities for third children, and subsidies for infertility treatment.

But whether these measures will lead to higher fertility rates is dubious, for a simple reason: they fail to tackle sufficiently the high economic hurdles that are causing South Koreans to delay or forego having children.

One of those hurdles is the cost of education. South Korean parents are willing to invest heavily in giving their few children the best chance of prospering. In 2015, they spent[3] almost 7% of their disposable income on private tutoring for their children in primary and secondary education. They also pay an absurdly high price for their children's college education, which no longer guarantees prosperity in life. In fact, South Korea's share of private spending for college education is the highest[4] among OECD countries, even ahead of the United States. That limits how many children parents may feel they can afford to raise.

For many young South Koreans, even marriage is economically unfeasible nowadays, owing to factors like high housing costs and youth unemployment, even among university graduates. The number of weddings in South Korea plunged from 435,000 in 1996 to 302,800 in 2015. In a country where only 2% of children are born outside marriage, this trend has a powerful impact on fertility rates.

Women confront the highest barriers to increased fertility. Pervasive gender inequality, together with a lack of affordable, high-quality childcare, causes many South Korean women to withdraw from the labor market after marriage or childbirth.

While men work long, inflexible hours, women assume the lion's share of the responsibility for family care. A 2014 survey[5] indicated that South Korean women spent, on average, three hours and 28 minutes daily on household activities and family care, compared to just 47 minutes for men, who also accounted for only 5.6% of those who took parental leave in 2015.

Though the new measures aim to boost this share, it will not be enough. After all, women are not just struggling to cope with uneven parental leave; many are leaving their jobs altogether after childbirth. And many of them do not wish to do so. In a recent survey[6] by the Federation of Korean Industries, 38% of the single female respondents said that they do not want children, mostly because they fear that they will struggle to keep up at work or lose their jobs. Only one-third responded positively to the government's program for promoting fertility.

South Korea's government must pursue a more comprehensive policy package aimed at lowering some of the barriers to childbirth. Women, in particular, need greater support, in order to eliminate the binary choice between career and family. The key is to provide more flexible work arrangements, to build a more accepting corporate culture, and to ensure accessible childcare, both public and private. To this end, allowing the migration of foreign housekeepers and caregivers could be very helpful.

South Korea remains conservative about offering permanent residency to foreign nationals. But the reality is that, in advanced economies where market services for childcare and households are available, highly educated women tend to have more children,[7] especially at older ages.

Japan, for its part, has managed to boost its ultra-low fertility rate —
which bottomed out[8] in 2005 at 1.26 — to 1.46 in 2015, through
consistent efforts to reduce childrearing costs and change the corporate
culture. To sustain this recovery, it has recently decided to take initiatives
to attract more foreign housekeepers. These changes reflect Prime
Minister Shinzo Abe's commitment to prevent the population from falling
below 100 million.

Even where foreign household workers do not raise the fertility rate,
they enable more women to continue working after having children. In
Singapore, for example, families often hire live-in maids from neighboring countries, including the Philippines and Indonesia, to take care of
the housework and childcare. Though Singapore's fertility rate stands at
just 1.3 — one of the lowest[9] in the world — this policy enables the
country to attract foreign talents to fill the population gap and sustain the
economy.

To some extent, demographic change is inevitable, as is its trans-
formative economic impact. But there are steps that governments can take
to shape demographic trends and blunt their negative effects. If South
Korea creates an environment in which families can live and work happily,
those families will grow larger.

Endnotes

Asia's Rebalancing Act

1. http://www.adb.org/sites/default/files/pub/2009/WP31-Decoupling-Recoupling.pdf
2. http://www.imf.org/external/pubs/ft/weo/2012/02/pdf/c4.pdf

India's Chinese Dream

1. http://data.worldbank.org/indicator/NY.GDP.MKTP.KD.ZG/countries/CN?display=graph
2. http://data.worldbank.org/indicator/BN.CAB.XOKA.CD/countries
3. http://data.worldbank.org/indicator/NY.GDP.MKTP.KD.ZG
4. http://data.worldbank.org/indicator/NY.GNP.PCAP.PP.CD
5. http://esa.un.org/wpp/
6. http://www3.weforum.org/docs/WEF_GlobalCompetitivenessReport_2013-14.pdf
7. http://data.worldbank.org/indicator/NV.IND.MANF.ZS
8. http://data.worldbank.org/indicator/SL.AGR.EMPL.ZS
9. http://www.project-syndicate.org/columnist/jagdish-bhagwati
10. http://www.project-syndicate.org/columnist/arvind-panagariya
11. http://www.mckinsey.com/insights/employment_and_growth/the_world_at_work

Starting South Korea's New Growth Engines

1. http://data.worldbank.org/indicator/NY.GNP.PCAP.CD
2. http://stats.oecd.org/Index.aspx?DataSetCode=EO
3. http://data.worldbank.org/indicator/SL.SRV.EMPL.ZS

4. http://www.asiaklems.net/
5. http://www.mckinsey.com/insights/asia-pacific/beyond_korean_style
6. http://www.adbi.org/working-paper/2014/07/18/6358.service.sector.productivity/

Containing China's Slowdown

1. http://www.imf.org/external/pubs/ft/weo/2015/update/02/pdf/0715.pdf
2. http://www.project-syndicate.org/columnist/lawrence-h--summers
3. http://www.frbsf.org/economic-research/events/2013/november/asia-economic-policy-conference/program/files/Asiaphoria-Meet-Regression-to-the-Mean.pdf
4. http://www.project-syndicate.org/commentary/china-2015-five-year-plan-by-justin-yifu-lin-2015-01
5. http://www.sciencedirect.com/science/article/pii/S0922142512000151
6. https://www.project-syndicate.org/commentary/are-services-the-new-manufactures-by-dani-rodrik-2014-10
7. http://econ.korea.ac.kr/~jwlee/papers/KLM_2015sept.pdf

Is South Korea Turning Japanese?

1. http://www.g8.utoronto.ca/finance/fm850922.htm
2. https://www.project-syndicate.org/columnist/shinzo-abe
3. http://www.imf.org/external/pubs/ft/weo/2015/02/
4. http://www.imf.org/external/pubs/ft/weo/2015/02/weodata/index.aspx
5. http://data.worldbank.org/
6. http://reports.weforum.org/global-competitiveness-report-2015-2016/

Maintaining the Emerging-Economy Growth Engine

1. http://data.worldbank.org/indicator/NY.GDP.MKTP.KD.ZG
2. https://www.imf.org/external/pubs/ft/weo/2015/02/weodata/index.aspx
3. https://www.piie.com/publications/wp/wp13-10.pdf
4. https://www.imf.org/external/pubs/ft/weo/2015/02/weodata/index.aspx
5. http://www.worldbank.org/content/dam/Worldbank/GEP/GEP2016a/Global-Economic-Prospects-January-2016-Spillovers-amid-weak-growth.pdf
6. http://pubdocs.worldbank.org/pubdocs/publicdoc/2016/1/991211453766993714/CMO-Jan-2016-Full-Report.pdf
7. https://www.project-syndicate.org/focal-points/goodbye-zirp

8. http://pubdocs.worldbank.org/pubdocs/publicdoc/2015/12/1770814495242 09011/PRN04-Dec2015-EmergingMarkets.pdf
9. http://www-wds.worldbank.org/external/default/WDSContentServer/WDSP/ IB/2014/11/13/000158349_20141113115057/Rendered/PDF/WPS7107.pdf
10. https://www.project-syndicate.org/focal-points/the-state-of-corruption
11. http://pubdocs.worldbank.org/pubdocs/publicdoc/2015/12/177081449524209011/ PRN04-Dec2015-EmergingMarkets.pdf

How Slow Will China Go?

1. http://data.worldbank.org/indicator/NY.GDP.PCAP.KD.ZG?locations=CN
2. http://data.worldbank.org/indicator/NE.GDI.TOTL.ZS?locations=CN
3. https://esa.un.org/unpd/wpp/Publications/Files/Key_Findings_WPP_2015.pdf
4. http://www.rieti.go.jp/en/database/CIP2015/index.html
5. http://www.frbsf.org/economic-research/events/2013/november/asia-economic-policy-conference/program/files/Asiaphoria-Meet-Regression-to-the-Mean.pdf
6. http://voxeu.org/article/china-s-growth-prospects
7. http://poseidon01.ssrn.com/delivery.php?ID=081001096020076068 091114001064117086033075065035019070107070097030004088065003 08811805610001802301505801710011210900200512101302105403506101 900900608209308309612612207000901502211709808902109809607108 0061120231071011140681020991180770281250060001060098&EXT=pdf
8. http://www.bis.org/statistics/totcredit.htm?m=6%7C326

Euro Lessons for East Asia

1. http://www.adbi.org/working-paper/2010/07/13/3938.chiang.mai.initiative.multilateralization/
2. http://www.amro-asia.org/

Financial Safety Nets for Asia

1. http://www.iie.com/publications/papers/truman12162011.PDF

Is North Korea Opening for Business?

1. https://www.cia.gov/library/publications/the-world-factbook/rankorder/2004rank.html
2. http://data.un.org/Data.aspx?d=SOWC&f=inID%3A18

China's New World Order

1. http://news.xinhuanet.com/english/business/2014-10/24/c_133740149.htm
2. http://www.imf.org/external/np/sec/memdir/members.aspx
3. http://www.adb.org/sites/default/files/page/30786/files/oi-appendix1.pdf
4. https://www.imf.org/external/np/sec/pr/2010/pr10418.htm
5. http://www.project-syndicate.org/columnist/shashi-tharoor
6. http://www.project-syndicate.org/commentary/china-silk-road-economic-belt-goals-by-shashi-tharoor-2014-10
7. https://www.devex.com/news/in-adb-s-image-china-led-aiib-to-test-infrastructure-alternative-in-asia-84280
8. http://www.reuters.com/article/2014/10/24/china-aiib-idINKCN0ID09520141024

Uniting for an Asian Century

1. http://www.imf.org/external/pubs/ft/weo/2016/02/weodata/index.aspx
2. https://www.adb.org/publications/asia-2050-realizing-asian-century
3. https://www.project-syndicate.org/commentary/north-korea-nuclear-tests-response-by-christopher-r-hill-2016-09
4. https://www.project-syndicate.org/commentary/asean-regional-security-threats-by-le-hong-hiep-2016-11

The Sino-Korean Trade War Must End

1. http://www.globaltimes.cn/content/1035359.shtml
2. https://unipass.customs.go.kr:38030/ets/
3. http://en.cnta.gov.cn/Statistics/TourismStatistics/201511/t20151104_750749.shtml
4. http://www.globaltimes.cn/content/1035359.shtml
5. https://www.project-syndicate.org/focal-points/a-korean-winter-is-coming

The Irresistible Rise of the Renminbi

1. http://www.imf.org/external/np/exr/facts/sdr.htm
2. http://www.bis.org/review/r090402c.pdf
3. https://global.oup.com/academic/product/exorbitant-privilege-9780199753789?cc=kr&lang=en&

Asia's View of the Greek Crisis

1. http://databank.worldbank.org/data/download/GDP.pdf
2. https://www.aei.org/publication/greek-lessons-imf/
3. http://www.nber.org/papers/w6680.pdf
4. http://www.piie.com/publications/wp/wp13-9.pdf
5. http://www.nber.org/chapters/c9654.pdf
6. http://www.imf.org/external/pubs/ft/scr/2015/cr15165.pdf

Closing Asia's Emerging Skills Gap

1. http://www.manpowergroup.com/wps/wcm/connect/408f7067-ba9c-4c98-b0ec-dca74403a802/2015_Talent_Shortage_Survey-lo_res.pdf?MOD=AJPERES&ContentCache=NONE
2. http://www.moe.go.kr/web/100085/site/contents/ko/ko_0120.jsp?selectId=1085
3. http://databank.worldbank.org/
4. http://link.springer.com/chapter/10.1007/978-94-007-5937-4_11
5. http://databank.worldbank.org/

The Way Back for Monetary Policy

1. https://www.project-syndicate.org/columnist/raghuram-rajan
2. https://m.rbi.org.in/Scripts/BS_SpeechesView.aspx?Id=993
3. https://www.project-syndicate.org/commentary/negative-rates-flawed-economic-model-by-joseph-e--stiglitz-2016-04
4. http://www.brookings.edu/blogs/ben-bernanke/posts/2016/04/11-helicopter-money
5. http://www.economics-ejournal.org/economics/journalarticles/2014-28
6. https://www.project-syndicate.org/commentary/coordinated-monetary-policy-revive-growth-by-kemal-dervis-2016-03
7. https://www.project-syndicate.org/commentary/monetizing-fiscal-deficits-benign-by-adair-turner-2016-03
8. http://www.brookings.edu/blogs/ben-bernanke/posts/2016/04/11-helicopter-money
9. http://www.g20.org/English/Documents/Current/201604/t20160427_2269.html

Taming the Chaebols

1. https://www.ft.com/content/1756e244-a1d7-11e6-82c3-4351ce86813f
2. http://beta.fortune.com/global500/samsung-electronics-13
3. http://www.mckinsey.com/global-themes/asia-pacific/beyond-korean-style
4. http://image.slidesharecdn.com/promoting-socially-inclusive-growth-oecd-economic-survey-korea-2016-160515163933/95/promoting-sociallyinclusive growthoecdeconomicsurveykorea2016-11-638.jpg?cb=1463374800

South Korea's Feminine Future

1. http://data.worldbank.org/indicator/NY.GDP.PCAP.CD
2. http://data.worldbank.org/indicator/SP.POP.DPND
3. http://www.oecd.org/inclusive-growth/Closing the Gender Gaps.pdf
4. http://www.korea.net/pdfcontent/news/Address_to_the_Nation--3-yr_Planfor_Economi.pdf
5. http://www.ilo.org/wcmsp5/groups/public/---ed_emp/---ifp_skills/documents/publication/wcms_232510.pdf#page=25
6. http://data.worldbank.org/indicator/SL.SRV.EMPL.ZS
7. http://www.project-syndicate.org/commentary/shinzo-abe-links-economic-recovery-in-japan-to-improved-prospects-for-global-peace-and-prosperity

China's Education Revolution

1. http://www.worldbank.org/en/news/press-release/2014/04/29/2011-international-comparison-program-results-compare-real-size-world-economies
2. http://www.nber.org/papers/w18673
3. http://www.barrolee.com/
4. http://www.oecd.org/pisa/46643496.pdf
5. http://www.oecd.org/pisa/keyfindings/PISA-2012-results-snapshot-Volume-I-ENG.pdf
6. http://esa.un.org/wpp/unpp/panel_indicators.htm
7. http://mckinseyonsociety.com/downloads/reports/Education/china-skills-gap.pdf
8. http://documents.worldbank.org/curated/en/2013/03/17494829/
9. http://mckinseyonsociety.com/can-china-close-the-skills-gap

Education and Opportunity

1. http://www.un.org/millenniumgoals/
2. http://www.barrolee.com/
3. http://www.barrolee.com/
4. http://www.sciencedirect.com/science/article/pii/S0922142512000187
5. http://timss.bc.edu/timss2011/
6. http://www.nber.org/papers/w15949

Asia's Almighty Middle Class

1. http://www.oecd.org/dev/44457738.pdf
2. http://www.brookings.edu/research/papers/2010/03/china-middle-class-kharas
3. http://www.worldbank.org/content/dam/Worldbank/document/China-2030-complete.pdf
4. http://ukcatalogue.oup.com/product/9780199379231.do

Can South Korea Make More Babies?

1. http://data.worldbank.org/indicator/SP.DYN.TFRT.IN?locations=KR
2. http://data.worldbank.org/indicator/SE.TER.ENRR.FE?locations=KR
3. http://blog.naver.com/moeblog/220638108940
4. https://data.oecd.org/eduresource/private-spending-on-education.htm
5. http://kostat.go.kr/portal/eng/pressReleases/1/index.board?bmode=read&bSeq=&aSeq=347182&pageNo=1&rowNum=10&navCount=10&currPg=&sTarget=title&sTxt=time
6. http://www.fki.or.kr/fkiact/promotion/report/View.aspx?content_id=334fdeab-004c-4c5a-b31e-388a585196ed&cPage=3&search_type=0&search_keyword=
7. http://onlinelibrary.wiley.com/doi/10.1111/ecoj.12148/full
8. http://data.worldbank.org/indicator/SP.DYN.TFRT.IN?locations=JP
9. http://data.worldbank.org/indicator/SP.DYN.TFRT.IN

Index

www.ingramcontent.com/pod-product-compliance
Lightning Source LLC
Chambersburg PA
CBHW071941260326
41914CB00004B/712